Don't Quit: The Best Things in Ministry Come Over Time
Published by Orange, a division of The reThink Group, Inc.
5870 Charlotte Lane, Suite 300
Cumming, GA 30040 U.S.A.
The Orange logo is a registered trademark of The reThink Group, Inc.

Other Orange products are available online and direct from the publisher. Visit our website at www.WhatIsOrange.org for more resources like these.

ISBN: 978-1-63570-056-5

Authors: Jessica Bealer & Gina McClain
Lead Editor: Mike Jeffries
Managing Editor: Steph Whitacre
Project Manager: Nate Brandt

Printed in the United States of America
First Edition 2017

3 4 5 6 7 8 9 10 11 12

03/10/18

DON'T QUIT

The Best Things In Ministry Come Over Time

Jessica Bealer and Gina McClain

For my dad who trusted me with my first ministry opportunity, my mom who lets me talk, vent, and dream, and my husband whose love and support motivates me daily.

Jessica

For my grandfathers who demonstrated what a lifetime of faith looks like, my parents who believed in me far more than I believed in myself, and my husband who has always been my biggest cheerleader. You didn't quit, so I won't either.

Gina

Authors' Note

As we brainstormed this book and its development—from the chapter ideas to the main points to the key takeaways—every conversation had a key individual in mind. **You.**

As ministry leaders, we are passionate about what we do and why we do it. And we've had the privilege of interacting with thousands of leaders like you who share that same passion.

Yet during our years in ministry, we've observed a trend across the landscape of leadership. Great leaders deciding to step away from the their calling.

It seems like every time you refresh your social media feed, a student or children's ministry leader is making an announcement that they've decided they just don't want to continue in church ministry. Next to their smiling avatar is the 140-character announcement with a blog link to more. It usually starts with a heading like, "God is moving our family!"

All the comments and replies to these posts celebrate what God is doing as another ministry leader uproots their influence, their skills, and their relationships to reinvest them elsewhere.

Here's the deal. We don't want to begrudge anyone who is following God's lead. We truly believe there are times when He moves you from here to there for a purpose. It's up to you to discern what He's doing and follow.

But we would suggest that more often a leader leaves under the banner of "God led me out," when the reality is they simply bumped into some challenges they can't seem to overcome.

Despite how much we wish it could be true, the raw passion that drove us into ministry may not be enough to keep us on track. There are far too many walls and ceilings we bump into. And if we lack the skills to navigate them, we find ourselves derailed, demotivated, and deeply frustrated. Soon, we start looking at other opportunities where the grass looks a lot greener. As this marinates in our minds, every unsuccessful outcome, dropped ball, or negative interaction is filtered through one question, "Am I still 'called' to be here? Or is God 'calling' me out?"

The driving motivation behind this project is the core belief that if God placed you in this role, then He has designed your skill set. He desires to move others closer to Him through you. He desires to develop others' potential through you. He has invited you to partner with Him in an amazing work.

But are you ready for that work?

Partnering with God in the work He is doing in others requires a teachable, malleable heart. It requires willingness to confront your own blind spots, being open to training and accountability, and humbling yourself to be coachable.

This is the cost of leadership. Are you ready to pay it?

In the pages of this book, we unpack some of the common challenges that leaders face in the realm of student's, children's, and next gen ministries. When handled poorly, these challenges can take you out of the ministry game. This project is a success only if it helps leaders to stay longer, dig deeper, and reap greater rewards than they ever imagined possible.

Now to Him who is able to do immeasurably more than all we ask or imagine, according to His power that is at work within us, to him be glory in the church and in Christ Jesus throughout all generations, for ever and ever! Amen (Ephesians 3:20 NIV).

INTRODUCTION

WRESTLING
WITH SUCCESS

Jessica Bealer

I n the span of six minutes, you could walk to get the mail, warm up leftovers for dinner, listen to a song, fold a load of towels, restock the copier with paper, or make a peanut butter and jelly sandwich. Then again, you could also defeat an Olympic legend and be the first American to take the gold medal in women's freestyle wrestling. That's exactly what Helen Maroulis decided to do with her six minutes at the 2016 Summer Olympics in Rio.

The day that happened, I was standing in the common area at work with 75 of my coworkers, watching and screaming at a massive television screen as we did our part to ensure Helen's victory from 5,000 miles away. I remember I was holding a pink Starbucks cake pop my husband had surprised me with. Helen was something to behold. From the first moment of the match to the last, she executed her skill to proficient perfection and defeated Yoshida in a decisive four to one victory. I hadn't even finished my cake pop.

I'm not a huge fan of women's wrestling. I don't know all the rules or the terminology. What drew me in that day was that Helen was one of ours—not only an American, but also a follower of Jesus. She had been training in Denver, and watching Elevation Church sermons from afar, worshiping with us online. She was one of us, the closest that most of us would ever get to experiencing athletic greatness. She was an Olympian.

A few weeks after her win, Helen came to church. I have to be honest, I geeked out a bit when she let me hold her gold medal. It was pretty cool. Yet even more astonishing than the gold medal was her story.

Helen started wrestling at age seven when her little brother joined a wrestling team and didn't have a partner. She stood in as his "dummy," but quickly realized her own love of the sport. Fast-forward nearly two decades to when Helen stood at the top of the Olympic podium. She got there by defeating Saori Yoshida, who held three Olympic gold medals and thirteen World Championship titles. She had taken down her own personal Goliath.

It wasn't fate, coincidence, or luck that propelled Helen to the top. It was willpower and faith. She believed if she made and executed a plan, found her identity in Christ, and worked harder than everyone around her, she could defeat the wrestling giant. She lived on chicken, spinach, avocado, and peanut butter. She worked on her technique and conditioning for nearly four hours a day, every day, and poured over years of film watching Yoshida's matches. She stayed hungry and humble.

In her first interview following her historic win, Helen was asked what she told herself before the match. She said, "Christ is in me, I am enough." What a bold statement. I was somewhat jealous of her confidence, envious of the enormity of her trust in Jesus. It wasn't until a few days after I met Helen that I began to realize her story was my story too.

I don't spend four hours a day in the gym, and I can assure you my diet is far more varied, but I do have a plan for the ministry I lead. I am committed to seeing that plan come to fruition, and I refuse to let idleness, ignorance, distraction, or doubt divert the call on my life. Christ is in me, I am enough. And the same is true for you.

The initiative you've shown by picking up this book tells of your commitment. I believe that the best is yet to come for you and your ministry, and I guarantee a life in ministry will be one of the most fulfilling journeys of your life. But this isn't a bait and switch. If you're just getting started, have been in this for a short time, or if you want to begin this coming Monday, there are a few things you should know before the starting pistol sounds.

YOU'LL WANT TO QUIT EVERY MONDAY MORNING. DECIDE NOW THAT YOU'LL STICK WITH IT.

There will be days you want to quit. I say it all the time, and I'll probably say it more than a few times in this book: *ministry is messy*. Our Savior is in the business of broken, hurting, confused, lonely, and insecure people. Parents doubt themselves—why wouldn't they doubt you? Volunteers' priorities will not always align with your own. Fellow staff members will both intentionally and unintentionally hurt your feelings. You'll want to quit every Monday morning. Decide now that you'll stick with it. If you wait until the heat of the moment to decide what to do, you'll always make the wrong decision. Commit now to enduring the tough days.

There will come a time when you'll want to barter the risk of greatness for the security of goodness. You'll find success. If you show up consistently and do what's been asked of you, I can guarantee you'll have wins along the way. But are a few small wins enough? Your ministry is either growing or dying. I often hear ministry leaders say, "We've just been in this season for a while," or "We're not growing in number, but we're growing in depth." I cringe when I hear sentiments like these.

Jesus told His disciples, "Therefore go and make disciples of all nations, baptizing them in the name of the Father and of the Son and of the Holy Spirit, and teaching them to obey everything I have commanded you" (Matthew 28:19–20a NIV). Yes, Jesus wants us to grow deeper in our faith. But it's not a coincidence He first spoke of sharing God's message with the world. If you want to go and make disciples, you are going to have to take some risks along the way. You will fail. People will be frustrated because you made a mistake. At times, you will question your calling, but don't sacrifice your mission for the security of the easily maintained. Take a risk and watch God move.

You are your biggest opponent. I can't tell you how many times I've beat myself up for a mistake made, a situation mishandled, or a promise forgotten. I can't tell you because the number is astronomically high. You will always have opposition, whether from a peer, an opinionated parent, a restraining budget, or the confines of church culture and tradition. You'll have enough obstacles along the way. Don't create additional ones by allowing your mind to wander to unhealthy places. At the first sign of mental attack, do something: pick up your Bible, play worship music, say a prayer, or call a friend. Contemplation is rarely the answer. Overthinking a problem can and will be the death of your ministry. Acknowledge you made a mistake, apologize if necessary, and let it go! You can't move on to tomorrow's victory if you're stuck in yesterday's dilemma.

Passion isn't always loud. In my position, I've had the opportunity to lead many types of leaders. One of my favorites is PJ. As a busy working mom, with a successful husband who frequently travels, PJ singlehandedly oversees the children's ministry at a campus of about 1,500 people in a rural area of Charlotte. PJ is what I call a ministry ninja, effective but quiet. Sometimes we assume success means being the loudest voice in the room with the flashiest personality. We believe in order to survive and be recognized, we have to dominate. However, if you seek life change for those that attend your church, hard work and dedication are the recipe for success. PJ doesn't do her job because she seeks recognition. She does her job because she loves the families she serves and the team she leads. Her passion shines through in the clarity of her emails, the organization of her resources, the level to which she executes her initiatives, and the endless hours she spends building relational equity with her team. Ask yourself if you are making a splash or if you are passionately pursuing the advancement of the kingdom.

Titles don't matter. Family ministry is not a stepping stone to something greater. An anointed calling into family ministry *is* something greater. This is my seventeenth year in family ministry. I started when I was just 19 years old. I didn't have a clue what I was doing. Actually, it was worse than that. I was the only daughter of the pastor of a startup church in rural East Tennessee. I knew nothing about kids, and even less about children's ministry. My dad came to me and asked if I wanted to be the Children's Director. I remember thinking, "Wow, that sounds important." And my first week on the job, I did feel important . . . right up until the moment the service was over and I was ready to hand back the kids and the impressive title. I felt clueless and unqualified. But I did learn a valuable lesson. A title does nothing if it's not supported with dedication, authenticity, and eagerness. Steward the opportunity God has given you. Serve Him with your whole heart in the role you've been assigned, and put the proverbial career ladder out of your mind.

Time is both your friend and your enemy. Between Gina and I, we've been in ministry for over three decades. That's a long time. Knowledge is power, but wisdom is priceless. The dilemma is that in order to gain the wisdom you need to be the best version of you, you need to have experience, but experience takes time. You may feel inadequate to face what's ahead, but if you stay hungry, remain humble, and push through the moments you feel like succumbing to doubt, the overwhelming days will become years, brimming with applicable insight.

Four years before her win in Rio, Helen Maroulis was expected to compete in the London Olympics. She entered the Olympic trials ranked No. 1 in the United States. She hadn't lost a match in 18 months. Then she lost to Kelsey Campbell in the best-of-three final. She was devastated, of course, but even more humbled when the Team USA coach asked her to go to London— not as a competitor, but as an assistant to the other wrestlers. When asked about her decision to serve as support for those who took her spot on Team USA, Helen said, "I didn't want to. I was heartbroken. But it's a great sport. It's going to teach you through the adversity. So I went." The adversity sharpened her focus. She changed weight class and powered on. If she hadn't, Rio wouldn't have become her reality. If she had thrown in the towel, it would have been Yoshida on top of the Olympic platform in 2016.

Every season has setbacks. The key to endurance is perception. When I look back at the last 16 years, I don't regret a moment. How could I? I've had the privilege of ministering to families from all over the globe. I've served alongside thousands of volunteers, and I've personally led 314 kids in prayers of salvation. These opportunities were not achieved because of intellect or capacity, they were earned through fortitude. When it comes to your first years in ministry, resilience is essential.

EVERY SEASON HAS SETBACKS. THE KEY TO ENDURANCE IS PERCEPTION.

How do you view what's hindering you? Will you allow your setbacks to suspend your efforts or sharpen your focus? If you're just starting this journey, let me break it down for you. Ministry isn't always easy, but it is fulfilling. It isn't always fun, but there are moments when your heart will burst with joy. There are tough days coming, but sweeter days to follow. You can't always choose your obstacle, but you can choose your response.

Are you ready?

1

CHAPTER

START WELL, NOT RIGHT

Gina McClain

"**W**ow! Who thought that was a good idea?"

The question slipped out before I realized what I was saying. I never meant to verbalize my thoughts. But it didn't matter. Whether I meant to or not, I'd spoken out of turn.

I was the new leader of my church's children's ministry. I was standing with my team, staring at an oddly shaped room with quirky accordion room dividers and mismatched fixtures, and the words fell out of my mouth. Everyone within earshot now knew how I felt about the general design of the environment. In eight brief words, I inadvertently discounted the work of those around me.

Those words had an immense impact on my new team. They reflected a part of my heart I'm ashamed to say was there. For some reason I thought I could do better. In that moment, I knew it didn't matter if what I said was true or not, statements like that weren't going to help me lead a team and ministry forward.

Can I be more transparent?

There was a time when I was so overconfident in my leadership ability that I would drive past churches along my daily route and think, "Oh, I could turn that ministry around. I could make that better." I truly believed I had the Midas touch—that no matter where I went, any ministry I led would turn to gold.

Arrogant, right?

I can't really tell you where this over-confident, over-compensating posture came from. Thankfully, time and experience have taught me the fallacy of it.

Over time, I began to realize success in ministry has less to do with a magic touch and more to do with a yielded heart. How I carried myself in that initial year of leadership would greatly determine how quickly and effectively I could create change.

After all, change has to happen. Increasing the capacity of any ministry often requires a transition in vision, strategy, and approach. It also requires next-level leadership. You're probably holding this book right now because you've been entrusted with the responsibility of being that kind of leader. And you've got what it takes!

But don't forget, leading change doesn't mean you rush in with guns blazing. Leading change requires a heart open to seeing what God has done so far, what He is doing now, and what He wants to do next. In order to do this successfully, there are three important postures leaders must maintain. These postures are: *honor past investments, get on the same page, and lead like a ninja warrior.*

HONOR PAST INVESTMENTS

Let's be real. When you step into a new ministry, there will be existing systems, environments, and processes that will make you scratch your head. Yet the things we see as ineffective today may have been effective in the past. Or it could be that the process you are questioning today was never effective. But in the end, it doesn't matter. At some point in time, there was a leader in place who implemented that system for a reason that made sense to them. That doesn't mean you have to keep it. It doesn't mean you can't ask questions about why it exists. But what if you filtered everything through the assumption that the model in place today was successful at some point?

This posture of honoring what's already in place doesn't prevent you from implementing change. But it does keep you from derailing the trust you're attempting to build with your new team.

As the newly appointed leader, you are standing on a bed of trust you haven't earned yet. It's been granted to you. It's your job to earn it over time. Trust is the currency of change. And you need lots of it.

Choosing to challenge the effectiveness of the model while honoring past investment tells your team that you see the hard work they've done. You see the blood, sweat, and tears that others have shed to get where you are today. You see the work of their hands, the investment of their hearts, and the great things that have happened as a result. Don't diminish it—honor it.

When you honor what's been done, others will more likely be open to trying new things in the future.

Try This: Do a 5 in 5.

Before making any changes, it's important to pinpoint what's going great. I have an exercise I do to help me focus on what's going well—I call it the "5 in 5." After an event or service, I invest five minutes writing down five things I witnessed that went right. I began doing this when I realized my focus was placed heavily on what was wrong, instead of seeing what was right. I needed to change my mindset to see what was going well in my new ministry. So I started doing this exercise every Monday morning. In the seasons that I'm faithful to this exercise, the level of celebration within the ministry is exponentially better.

Here's an example of my most recent 5 in 5:

1. Dave, an elementary small group leader, was intentional in how he engaged one of his few who came into our environment acting standoffish. The little boy wasn't interested in leaving dad and joining his small group. Dave was quick to respond, gentle in his encouragement, and respectful of the boy's parents. The effort paid off. Well done!

2. Our stage host was called into work for an emergency. Another volunteer, Bobby, was prepared to cover the role. Bonus: Bobby had an awesome attitude about the last-minute change.

LEADING CHANGE
DOESN'T MEAN YOU
RUSH IN WITH GUNS
BLAZING. LEADING
CHANGE REQUIRES
A HEART OPEN TO
SEEING WHAT GOD
HAS DONE SO FAR,
WHAT HE IS DOING
NOW, AND WHAT HE
WANTS TO DO NEXT.

3. Kim was so flexible when more kids than expected showed up on Saturday night. Her attitude and ability to adjust exemplified the model volunteer. I loved it!
4. The nursery team was encouraging to a new couple leaving their baby for the first time. They took time to lead the couple through what to expect. Great job!
5. Harley rocked it as a worship leader. She's a great addition to the team.

GET ON THE SAME PAGE

You were placed at the helm of your ministry because your leader believes you are capable of leading it forward. But it's dangerous to assume your game plan is the same as theirs. It's tough to build a skyscraper on a foundation designed for a house.

Before you implement any changes, invest the time and energy necessary to ensure your game plan aligns with those who lead you. Programming or events that aren't integrated into the overall vision of the church are divisive and unproductive, no matter how amazing they might be. There are few churches in existence that are swimming in resources like time, money, physical space, and volunteers. (For the ministry leader that has more resources than they know what to do with, let me just say *congratulations*. You're the minority.)

So we've got to be strategic with the resources available. The first step is to find out how your ministry feeds into the greater vision of the church. Take time to discover how programming and events born out of your ministry move your church closer to seeing that vision become reality.

This sounds great in theory. It's very challenging in practice.

Can you guess why it can be difficult? Because we like our ideas! We're personally attached to them. But we won't serve our churches well if we implement ideas that cause us to drift from the overall vision.

In my early years of ministry, I fell in love with big production

events. I still love the music, the lights, and the crowds. In my
mind, the bigger, the better. Maybe your church hosts an FX
(Family Experience) for families in your community. If so, you
know that big events are a ton of work, but they're also a ton of
fun.

If you visited my church (Faith Promise) on a weekend, it
might appear on the surface that we're driven by big, concert-
like worship events. But the truth is, small groups are the
engine that keep us moving. We believe small groups are the
most strategic method through which people can grow. So
as much as I love stage-driven events, if my agenda was to
create productions that draw families in, yet I focused little
on connecting them to small groups, then I'd be working
against the very strategy my church has employed to reach our
community.

In order for my ministry strategy to align with the strategy of
my church's overall approach, small groups have to be a high
priority, not a second thought. So we invest a lot of resources
and time into making small groups successful. Don't get me
wrong, we still do large events with amazing worship, crazy
lights, and creative storytelling. But we do these events to
mobilize kids and their parents toward a next step of connecting
with one another and with a church community.

There's nothing wrong with having ideas and preferences when
it comes to ministry. In fact, you were probably hired for this
job because you have great ideas! But you won't get very far if
your ideas and preferences don't align with the leaders who have
been placed above you.

A solid move for getting on the same page with leadership is to
become a student of those to whom you report. Find out what
they see for the future, what direction they want to take, and
how your ministry plays into that. Then discern where you can
shape your strategy to align with the overall direction of the
church.

Try This: Play a game of "Ask Your Leader."
If you're wondering what the leader above you is thinking, then take a moment and ask your direct report if they'd be willing to set up a time to chat with you. When you get together, ask the following questions:

- What are two critical outcomes you want to see from my ministry?
- What's your expectation for when these outcomes will be met?
- What are the non-negotiables in our ministry in terms of programming, environments, and strategy?

LEAD LIKE A NINJA WARRIOR

My family is a big fan of the show *American Ninja Warrior*. We get downright giddy when a new episode airs. There's something about the impossibility of the challenges and the sheer grit required to complete them. The doorframes of my living room are covered in the footprints of my 11-year-old. He simply can't help himself. Watching the ninjas traverse the course on television inspires him so much that doorframes now double as spider walls. It's impressive to see him run, jump, and brace himself in the narrow space.

I think the thing I love most about the ninja course is that despite its challenges, the course can be conquered with training and focus. But no one jumps from the first challenge (the floating steps) to the final challenge (the invisible ladder) in one leap. The course is conquered one challenge at a time.

Leading your team through change is the same.. You don't introduce change and see the fruit of that change, all in one step. You actually have to overcome a series of challenges along the way. And not only do you have to conquer each challenge, you are simultaneously leading another group of ninjas to victory as well.

The only way to accomplish this is to ensure you lead your team by providing defined direction and giving clear steps to guide the way. This is where vision and values come into play.

Defined Direction

In *American Ninja Warrior*, it's the buzzer that signifies when a competitor has reached the end of the course. If they don't hit a buzzer, the ninja knows there are still challenges ahead. They haven't reached their goal. Your ministry team needs to know the same thing. They need to know when they've hit their goal. Even though ministry is never done, creating celebration points along the way gives your team the energy to charge ahead. You need to cue your team for when it's time to hit that buzzer with all their might and dance around like crazy people.

Knowing the value Faith Promise placed on small groups, the direction this ministry needed to lean toward was a stronger small group culture. But the journey ahead could get rocky. Recruiting the number and caliber of volunteers necessary seemed like an impossible climb up the warped wall. So, we had to figure out how to celebrate the little "buzzers" along the way.

As a leader, where can you place markers to stop and celebrate another step in the right direction? How can you ensure there is ample celebration around the critical steps that lead you to see your mission come to reality?

Clear Steps

I love the idea of "ninja holds." Nearly every challenge on *American Ninja Warrior* involves gripping some version of a handhold in order to traverse the course. Often the holds are difficult and challenge the participant to focus with great effort. If the holds were too easy or too close together, there would be no challenge to it. The course would lose its appeal. If anyone could do it, the course would lose the quality that sets the ninja competitors apart from the rest of humanity.

On the flip side, if the holds were too spread out or impossible to grab, competitors would give up. And no one would successfully complete the challenge.

Your ministry has leaders. Hopefully strong ones. And you want to lead your leaders well. The best way to lead them is to give them ninja holds that challenge them to focus their efforts and stretch their abilities, yet reward them along the way.

In the ministry world, ninja holds are clear vision and strategy. Great vision without solid strategy is nothing short of frustrating. Yet one of the first holes a leader can step in is to share a great vision with no plan for how to get there.

Creating a strategy is like creating a series of ninja holds that lead others through the challenges of ministry. Obviously our objective is a strategy many can follow. So the level of difficulty has to be appropriate. Don't be tempted to make things easy. The greater the challenge, the greater the value.

Try This: Map out your direction.

Invest time getting your plans out of your head and on paper. Now that you're on the same page with your leadership, what is the best next step for your ministry? Is it to introduce an FX event to engage families in a common experience? Is it to dig deeper into small groups to ensure every kid has the best seat in their circle?

Define the direction of your ministry in this new season. Then clarify the steps needed to make it a reality. If your volunteers understand the direction you are headed and the steps to get there, they'll find it easier to follow.

KNOW YOUR INFLUENCERS

I'd been in my role for six months. It was time for a volunteer training to bring the team on board with the new focus on small groups in our preschool and elementary environments. I was super excited about the plan for that Saturday morning. I would lead the whole group with the vision of small groups then send everyone off to area-specific breakouts. I'd carefully chosen some highly competent volunteers to lead these breakouts and share great tips and tricks for leading in preschool and elementary environments. I walked away that afternoon like I'd hit a homerun. Success!

On the drive home, I received a call from one of my preschool small group leaders. "Hey Gina, I just wanted you to know what was shared in our breakout today. I don't think it's what you'd hoped for."

It took me a while to digest what the volunteer had shared. But in the course of that 45-minute breakout, my preschool breakout leader single-handedly dismantled the vision I'd so passionately shared just moments before.

To be fair, her intentions were pure. This person had invested more hours in preschool ministry as a volunteer than I could count. She was committed and passionate to say the least. However, she didn't align with the direction I was headed. And I never took the time to figure that out.

I think leading leaders is one of the trickiest parts of leadership.

So far we've talked about honoring the foundation you're building upon, aligning your plans with the vision of the church, and creating a clear pathway for others to follow you toward a ministry vision.

Your next critical step is to bring the right people around you to reach that vision. And finding the right people is a matter of identifying your Influencers and determining which ones have influence you want to amplify and which ones have influence you need to manage.

Let's get down to the nitty-gritty. What's an Influencer? Influencers are the volunteers that others follow. Their opinions carry more weight than others. They have the ability to sway others toward or away from your vision.

In a season of change, it's important that you know who your Influencers are and what kind of impact they have on your team.

I like to use a graph to map out my Influencers. This map helps me identify whose influence I want to leverage and whose influence I need to manage.

The graph is simple. Draw out a graph defining the y-axis as

"Flexibility" and the x-axis as "Competence." Then create a list
of all the Influencers you have on your volunteer team. As you
plot them on the graph, answer the question, "How flexible and
competent is this leader?"

Each volunteer will land in a different spot on the graph, but
you'll find a great opportunity to work strategically with your
team. Take a look at the variety of Influencers and the kind of
impact they can have.

The Resilient Cheerleader
Some of your Influencers are high on the flexibility side, but
low on the competence side. They've gained their influence with
their contagious energy and "can-do" attitude. They will do
anything you ask them to do. But they may not be able to pull it
off. When you ask others to follow these leaders, you may create
frustration. Your volunteers want to know that the person you
empower to lead is capable of the job you've given them. If they
aren't, you quickly lose the confidence of that team.

The Skillful Stick in the Mud
Other Influencers are more competent, but less flexible. These
leaders will struggle to buy into the changes you propose and
pulling them forward may feel like dragging a mule. When you
ask others to follow these leaders, you may find an entire team
moving in a direction you don't want them to go because you've
empowered a leader that isn't aligned with you. The temptation
is too great to insert their own opinion and perspective on the
directives within the ministry. Left unchecked, you'll find an
entire team of people who have disengaged from the vision and
are functioning in a silo.

The Game Changer
The key Influencers you really want to leverage are the
highly competent, highly flexible types. These leaders are not
doormats. They won't hang on every word you say. They'll
ask hard questions and have high expectations. But they will
support you and the changes you propose. Their competence has
already earned the respect of others. Their support of you and
the direction you lead will encourage others to follow. These are

the volunteers with influence you want to leverage. These are
your game changers.

The Passive Laggard

What about the final quadrant? Great question. Truth be told,
you shouldn't have any Influencers in the low-competence, low-
flexibility corner. Because they don't really have any influence.

Now you might have one or two of these on your volunteer team.
But they should be the exception, not the rule. In fact, they
should be "that" volunteer who just can't seem to find their fit in
your ministry. Why? Because your ministry is filled with vision-
driven volunteers that are not content unless they are winning.
A ministry filled with vision-driven volunteers will actually repel
someone who cannot latch onto the vision. It's as irritating as
sandpaper.

So, watch out for the Passive Laggard. Don't fight to hang on to
them, no matter how empathetic you might feel. They do more
damage than good and your Game Changers simply won't work
with them.

Identifying these Influencers and how to leverage their influence
will equip you to lead more strategically. With every change you
implement, there are some important steps to take to provide
direction and handholds to each type of Influencer.

STEP 1: KEEP GAME CHANGERS IN THE KNOW

Address your Game Changers first. Bring them in the loop early.
Give them space to learn, ask questions, pick apart ideas, and
help you strategize. Their support will accelerate the rate of
change in your ministry.

STEP 2: PREP YOUR SKILLFUL STICKS IN THE MUD

These Influencers need to be in the know, but it's important to
be strategic with how. Giving them space to digest change can
go a long way. Pull them aside and give them space to process
their thoughts. Let them ask questions, express doubts, or
vent frustrations. When you do this, ask them to agree that
frustrations and concerns should be voiced specifically with you

	High	
	Flexibility	Low
High	**Competence**	
	Low	

High Competence, High Flexibility = Game Changer

Low Competence, High Flexibility = Resilient Cheerleader

High Competence, Low Flexibility = Skillful Stick in the Mud

Low Competence, Low Flexibility = Passive Laggard

and not with the general public. Give them access to you, as this
will prevent them from creating their own pathway to disagree.
Make sure they know the critical nature of trust and team.
If they can't support the change, they don't need to continue
leading.

These conversations can be difficult, and I don't know anyone
who enjoys them. But in my experience, I've never regretted
having the conversation. However, I've certainly regretted not
having it, so be sure to make talking with these Influencers a
priority.

STEP 3: RALLY THE RESILIENT CHEERLEADER
After you've brought your Game Changers and Skillful Sticks
in the loop, it's time to rally your Resilient Cheerleaders. These
are your Influencers who bring energy and excitement to the
change. They will help you create momentum and sway the
majority in the right direction.

STEP 4: LET THE PASSIVE LAGGARDS GO
If you really want to make a change, you'll need the right people
on board. And you'll need the wrong people, well, not on board.
The Passive Laggard might be a great person with the potential
to be an amazing volunteer in a different ministry or role. Now
is the time to have a gentle conversation with your volunteers
who might not be a great fit for your ministry about how to
help them find success elsewhere. You never know, you might
lead them to a role that inspires them to be a game changer for
someone else's team!

These steps will help you identify your Influencers, recognize
how to leverage or manage their influence, and set you up to
create momentum behind the change you want to make.

These initial steps in leading your ministry can be tricky. But
if you can honor investments, get on the same page, lead like
a ninja warrior, and identify your Influencers, you are well on
your way to building the ministry you wish you walked into.

2

CHAPTER

BIG
ASKS
VS.
SMALL TASKS

Jessica Bealer

I f you're reading this book, you're not the typical volunteer or staff member. You probably think about ministry conundrums when you're in the shower and evaluate systems during your drive time. You spend your Saturday evenings at the Christian bookstore or in the toy aisle at Target. Ministry is in your DNA. It's who you are. You're what I call a Ministry Lifer. Welcome to the club. You're in for a sometimes bumpy, often chaotic ride that will hopefully be one of the most rewarding experiences of your life.

For Ministry Lifers like us, there's no task too big, too small, or too gross. I've scrubbed floors, cleaned toilets, organized drawers, and cut cardstock in every shape known to man. I've slept on a toddler table, gone consecutive days without a shower, consumed energy drinks to stay awake, and survived on Cheetos and Dr. Thunder (the less expensive, ministry-budget-friendly version of Dr. Pepper). Why? Because that's what you do when you're a Ministry Lifer. You do whatever it takes to point others to Jesus.

You're not clueless. You know that your brand of insanity is unique. What you're maybe not aware of is that most people yearn for the type of calling you sense daily. Steven Furtick, pastor of the church where I served as a staff member for several years, was inspired at the age of 16 by this line in Jim Cymbala's book *Fresh Wind, Fresh Fire*: "I despaired at the thought that my life might slip by without seeing God show Himself mightily on our behalf." We all wish to lead a life of greater purpose, a life where God shows his power and strength on our behalf. Your volunteers are no different. They wish to be part of a movement bigger than themselves. For this reason, many are willing to set aside personal preferences and make sacrifices.

When we understand this, it changes the way we communicate with our teams. There's nothing wrong with delegation. More than 95 percent of what happens on the weekends at churches across America is possible because of the investment of incredible volunteers. When I was on staff at Elevation Church, there were more than 2,200 children's ministry volunteers. With each one of them, I saw that people crave serving opportunities that provide them with a clear vision and an understanding of their contribution.

God has big plans for His church and He's willing to use anyone to accomplish them. The only requirement is obedience. But how can we inspire people to act in obedience to God? We first have to remind ourselves that we're not requesting that volunteers be obedient to us as leaders or to a set of policies and procedures put forth by church administrators. We want those serving alongside us to act upon the unique and special gifting God has given them. Then we must draw a direct correlation between need and skill set.

Too many times when we see a problem, our solution is to throw the closest available volunteer at it, whether or not that person has the right skill set. After all, it takes more time and effort to identify the *best* person for a job. So instead, we often go for the first person available. God desires for every one of His children to draw closer to Him through service and when you take the time to connect people to His purpose, you'll see ministry happen before your eyes. When you find the right person for the right assignment working *in* the ministry, will actually *be* ministry in and of itself. When people see what God can do through them, their level of commitment will astound you.

Once you've identified the best person on your team for a particular assignment, it's important to communicate what you need in a way that will inspire action. I used to live close to a shopping mall with a Thomas Kinkade gallery. I vividly remember visiting the gallery and being awed by the beautiful pieces of artwork. They were striking from a distance, but there was something about each piece that made me want to draw near and look at every detailed brush stroke. Ministry is the same.

Ministry is all about life change—seeing people far from God experience fulfillment through the love of Christ, watching children grow as they're exposed to the teachings of Jesus, and seeing students transformed by the acceptance and companionship they find with like-minded teens. That's the big picture. It's beautiful and inspiring.

But when you step closer, you see millions of small sacrifices, people just like those on your team carrying out small tasks and finding ways to selflessly give of themselves to see God's plan come to fruition. Lesson plans get stapled, sound systems get repaired, walls get painted, and snacks get purchased. Ministry happens in the *small tasks*. But it's easier to inspire people when you paint the big picture first. I call this *making a big ask*.

As you look at the big picture of your ministry, it's easy to see it in increments of small tasks. After all, you're the leader because you see all the details. But if you want to inspire those you lead, you'll want to change your focus from assigning small tasks to making big asks. Here's an example of the difference between the two:

Small Tasks: "Would you go into each of the toddler classrooms and clean the counters, take out the trash, vacuum, and straighten the toys?"

Big Ask: "We're going to have a lot of first-time guests this weekend. We want to exceed parents' expectations by going above and beyond to have our toddler rooms be clean and safe. Would you be willing to go room to room and use your detailed eye to make them look amazing?"

Do you see the difference? The first question is just a list of tasks. The second not only speaks to the vision of the ministry and explains why it's necessary to clean those rooms, but it also relays a level of trust. It says, "I trust you to identify the problem areas and fix them without supervision." In my early years of ministry, I frequently messed this up. I felt like if I didn't spell it out, it wouldn't get done. What I failed to realize is that micromanaging can actually do more harm than good.

CONSISTENT SERVICE BUILDS CHARACTER, BUT IT ALSO INCREASES PRODUCTIVITY AND QUALITY. WHEN YOU PRAISE EFFORT, IT SETS PRECEDENT. IT ENCOURAGES DEPENDABILITY AND DEEPENS DEDICATION.

When I control the details, I leave no room for ownership. I'm often blown away by how, when I take time to explain to a teammate the vision behind a project, that person will take it to a whole other level, exceeding all my expectations. Collaboration conveys trust and trust builds relational equity.

Just because you've painted the big picture, cast vision, and placed your trust in the hands of the right person doesn't always mean there won't sometimes be disappointment. We're all human. We make mistakes. In the first decade of my ministry, I got it wrong more often than I got it right. Your team will probably be no different. They won't always exceed your expectations. Sometimes an assignment will fall short of your expectations. How many times have you asked someone to do something and then waited for him or her to leave the building so you could go fix it? We've all been there. Yet despite missteps, you should always praise a team member or volunteer for their efforts, despite the results.

Consistent service builds character, but it also increases productivity and quality. What was acceptable the last time might not feel right the next. When you praise effort, it sets precedent. It encourages dependability and deepens dedication. I will always prefer a dependable, dedicated volunteer who occasionally doesn't get "it" right over perfection that comes at the cost of my joy and hours spent away from my family. Ministry is more easily accomplished with reinforcements. I've thrown a lot at you, so let's take a moment to review.

First, identify the *best*—not the first available—person on your team to complete the task or assignment.

Then, make the big ask. Avoid giving the individual a list of small tasks.

Next, cast vision, leaving room for interpretation.

Finally, offer praise for their efforts, not the results.

In the book *Creating a Lead Small Culture*, Reggie Joiner says,

"Maybe your leaders aren't committed because you haven't asked them to commit to something significant." Is your ministry significant? Is this calling important? If so, share the *why* behind the *what*. I am convinced that volunteers will go to any length when motivation intersects purpose. As a Ministry Lifer, you understand the joy and fulfillment that comes when you see God move through you. Now it's time to bring others along for the journey.

3

CHAPTER

PROVE IT

Jessica Bealer

To pray or not to pray? That was the question. The answer seems obvious. Prayer is always a good thing, right? Let me give you context.

Once a quarter, in the elementary-age programming at Elevation Church, the plan of salvation is presented. Kids are taught what it means to be a follower of Jesus and given the opportunity to make that choice for themselves. For the first six years of our ministry, we followed the same protocol. It probably looked similar to methods you've seen before. Kids would express a desire to follow Jesus during the presentation. We would then separate them from the group, lead them in the prayer of salvation, tell mom or dad of the decision during pick-up, and send each child home with a new, age-appropriate Bible.

About four years ago, we began to hear a repeating theme among parents. They would say something like, "Oh! That's great. I just wish I could have been there," or "I've been answering a lot of questions lately. I thought this day was coming." They would offer a watery smile, hug their child, and head to the car. This same interaction happened so often we began to question our process. Were we doing a disservice to parents by cutting them out of this special moment in their child's life? Were we limiting the impact of the decision by not including the most important influencer in the process?

Nearly the entire children's ministry team was in favor of waiting for mom or dad to say the prayer of salvation. I was not convinced. At this point, I'm going to be honest and vulnerable with you. I thought the idea would blow up in our faces. The change was going to be messy. There were too many unanswered questions. How would we identify those kids and parents we needed to pull aside during pick-up? Where would these conversations and prayers happen? Who would lead them? What if the child came with a friend and mom or dad wasn't present? What if mom and dad weren't believers themselves?

My reluctance came from a place of fear and lack of confidence. If any member of our staff or volunteer teams mishandled this new and very intricate process, a child could miss the opportunity to give his or her life to Jesus. Just writing that last sentence makes me anxious. I often wish there was a ministry supermarket. In this imaginary store, I could swing by on my way home from work, pick up a couple extra pairs of helping hands, a bigger budget, and a family-size vat of discernment.

Unfortunately for you and me, no such superstore exists. However, I've discovered that most individuals gifted with discernment were not born with it. It's a skill that developed over time through observation, evaluation, and a willingness to seek counsel when necessary. In my quest for answers, I asked my husband for guidance. He shared a practical process that helps him identify effective solutions prior to implementation, thus avoiding unnecessary setbacks, expenses, and wasted effort. The point of the process is to PROVE your suppositions— or, in many cases, disprove them. It's not a foolproof plan, but it does provide a concrete way to measure what would otherwise be speculation. Let's take a look at the PROVE IT method.

PROBLEM
Ask yourself: What's the problem I'm trying to solve?

This is where you get specific. What is the actual question that needs to be answered or predicament that needs to be solved? It may feel bigger or smaller than it actually is. It's not enough to say, "Our ministry isn't growing." There isn't a solution for that problem. It's too big, too vague. The PROVE IT method requires you to go deeper. Problems are a lot like banana pudding, you may have to dig through several layers to get to what's fundamentally at the center of it all. I'm talking about the Nilla Wafers. Everyone knows those cookies are the key ingredient. If your ministry isn't growing, you need to start by spending a generous amount of time working through each layer until you can clearly identify an origin. "Our ministry isn't growing," becomes "Our first time guest retention is less than nine percent." That's a problem just waiting for a solution.

RESULT
Ask yourself: What does success look like?

The reason we must define the problem is so we can clearly distinguish the win. If the problem is vague, you'll never get started, but if the objective is blurry, you'll never finish. Knowing where you're going is just as important as knowing what's wrong when it comes to initiating change successfully. No one gets in the car headed for vacation and says, "Let's just go. We'll figure out where we're going as we drive." Your final destination must be programmed into the GPS. Otherwise you'll get lost in the mountains of frustration and take an exit called complacency. I want more for my ministry. I want results.

OPTIONS
Ask yourself: What are all of the possible options?

One of the best places to start when searching for a new system or strategy is the sky. Let me explain. Through the years, I've found that one of the largest obstacles to accomplishing a goal is the weight I give to my own opinion. I tend to be decisive. If you ask me a question, you'll get an answer. Generally, it'll sound like a viable option, but that's the issue. It's one viable option. When evaluating strategies, it's wise to have several viewpoints with differing perspectives. A blue-sky meeting is one in which key players committed to the process and willing to challenge and compromise gather in an idea-friendly space and put forth ideas for the sake of diligence and innovation. Lofty ideas are welcome, but so is candor. A blue-sky meeting requires imagination and thick skin. This step is key to unlocking potential by embracing your limitations and imagining what is possible.

VARIABLES
Ask yourself: What variables impact the problem?

I would define variables as worries, or as the things that keep you up at night. Every solution has variables—things that could change and instantly alter or nullify your strategy. Sometimes your influence can help to reduce their effect, but more often than not, they are outside your control. It's important to examine all possibilities that could impact your strategy or initiative and verbalize them. The monster in the corner looks a lot less intimidating in the light of day when you realize you were scared of a coat stand. Once you've listed the variables, appraise them. Decide what you're comfortable with and what would derail the mission. Rarely have I achieved a goal in which everything went right. Variables are the factors that are liable to change. The best initiatives come to terms with the inevitable and make a plan to counter the effects.

EXPENSE
Ask yourself: What is the cost in terms of money, hours, and people?

In many situations the cost is apparent. In others, you may have to "play it out" and make estimations to fully grasp the expense or manpower required to see a particular solution implemented. However, this last step is crucial in realizing the viability of your chosen strategy. If the expense is too high, it employs more volunteers than you have available, or it doesn't fit inside your timetable, it may be necessary to tweak your strategy or scrap it all together. Don't be afraid to PROVE an idea over and over again until you get it right.

When my team and I looked at the salvation prayer issue through the lens of the PROVE IT method, we found clarity. We were able to get to the root of our hesitancy and fear. We identified a successful outcome, which was a family who felt loved and included in our ministry, and a child who made the most important decision of his or her life in the presence of those who will love and support him or her for years to come.

We narrowed our options and examined all the variables. We also came to a clear understanding of the ramifications of our decision, and even though it didn't make implementation of the new strategy any easier, it did prepare us for all possible outcomes. In the end, we decided to include parents in that crucial moment of prayer from that point forward.

Although we came to a very logical and well thought-out decision, God moved in a miraculous way. The results of the change were nothing short of supernatural. Over the past four years, I've seen moms and dads burst into tears of gratitude. I watched as a young father, a new believer himself, tentatively made his way through the salvation prayer that he had spoken aloud only moments before in the main auditorium. I witnessed an entire family of five follow in their son's and brother's examples and say the salvation prayer for the first time as a family. [1]

The PROVE IT method isn't infallible. However, as I mentioned earlier, if discernment is a skill developed over time through observation, evaluation, and a willingness to seek direction when necessary, then the best way to work on this area of spiritual development is to observe, evaluate, and work through hot topics with those you love and trust.

In the life of your ministry you will rarely experience seasons short of problems or mishaps. Overtime, you'll develop a level of discernment that enables you to make crucial assessments with decisiveness. As with anything, when you have a plan and intentionally pursue growth you'll progress. It won't happen overnight, but I do believe that perspective and discernment are yours for the taking if you'll only PROVE IT!

---

1   To learn more about this approach, check out Orange's Family Birthday Celebration resources, available in the Orange Store.

4

CHAPTER

BALANCE
IN MINISTRY
. . .
(AND
OTHER FUNNY
JOKES)

Gina McClain

I t was the biggest event of the summer. Our week-long Vacation Bible School culminated in a family worship night to celebrate the week. The energy of this event was always off the charts. But the hours invested to pull it off were ridiculously high.

I hadn't been in my role more than a few weeks and my kids were still adjusting to our new family rhythm. Planning and preparing for the event had already kept me from home most nights, so when my son decided he wanted to bring his cousin to the family worship night, I wanted to do everything I could to make that happen.

It was all carefully planned. Leave the office in time to pick my son up from school, swing over to my nephew's house and grab him, roll through the drive-thru for a super-healthy meal of nuggets and fries, then crash land at the church in time for volunteers to show up.

It was a well-laid plan that went astonishingly wrong from the beginning. I didn't anticipate the volunteer that needed to give me a detailed explanation as to why the craft for the night wouldn't work with the materials we provided.

I didn't plan for the parent stalling in the pick-up line because her child couldn't buckle his seat belt.

Or the drive-thru line to be so busy.
Or traffic to be so congested.

I walked into the church well after my volunteer team had arrived. In a post-mortem meeting, the children's pastor I served under made it abundantly clear that my late arrival could not happen again. I could do nothing more than agree with him. No argument. I looked him square in the eyes and told him, "It will never happen again."

I walked away feeling like the biggest failure. I'd let my volunteers down, let my children's pastor down, and was convinced I'd let the ministry down. Internally I determined I would never let that happen again.

The problem is, I overcorrected. To avoid the perception that I wasn't giving enough to the ministry I served, I introduced unhealthy work habits. I arrived earlier and worked later each weekend, leaving my husband to shuffle our three kids to and from weekend activities with little to no help from me. Though I knew the hours I worked were excessive, working less just didn't seem an option. I mean, how else would I get everything done?

I had to own up to it. I knew this wasn't sustainable. So I fought to pursue the unattainable goal of achieving work-life balance. I tried to create boundaries around family time and ministry responsibilities. I would squeeze to-do list items into carefully apportioned hours of the day. I wrestled with requests for my time that fell outside my "regular" ministry hours.

These requests were for good things—great things even. But they were additional pulls on already limited family time. So I tried the "comp time" approach. If an event required additional time during the week, I'd then attempt to balance things by pulling time from somewhere else in my work schedule. But there were always additional events or projects happening that demanded more of my time and attention. I quickly learned stealing time from my regular work to execute extra events meant my administrative work never got done.

I think the fallacy of work-life balance is just that: a myth. Like a unicorn. So rare and so fleeting, it's exhausting to chase. The problem is, an inability to achieve balance may lead you to believe your aren't cut out for ministry.

Let's take a moment to accept reality. You're already in ministry. You're probably aware work-life balance doesn't exist. As long as you're shepherding volunteers, partnering with parents, and mentoring the next generation, your job will never be 9-to-5. So stop trying to fit a square peg in a round hole.

Maybe you're wondering: *Is there another way to view the flow of ministry in our lives? Is it possible to have a different, healthier perspective on ministry and it's pull on who we are?*

The intent of the message of work-life balance is pure and good. To grow and thrive into all God made you to be, there has to be a distinction between who you are as a Christ-follower and who you are as a ministry leader.

However, the key is the difference between distinction and separation. The two terms are so similar it is hard to tell the difference. But follow me for a moment as we look at their dictionary definitions.

Distinction (dih-**stingk**-shuh n):
the recognizing or noting of differences

Separation (sep-uh-**rey**-shuh n):
a place, line, or point of parting

The term *distinction* recognizes differences between two or more things. The term *separation* is the very act of pulling two or more things apart.

I don't know about you, but I have the toughest time keeping my personal life separate from my ministry life. It's simply impossible.

The world we operate in has a 24/7 rhythm. Though we have defined work hours, rarely does ministry fit neatly within that schedule. You might put in a full work day planning for the next big event, cleaning up after your mid-week service, and prepping for Sunday.

Yet even when your day is done, you may still . . .
>
> take a call from a volunteer while you're picking up groceries.
>
> drop a meal off on the way to soccer practice for the mom that just had a baby.
>
> stop by the hospital after piano lessons to visit one of the kids from your small group.

Ministry is busy. Your personal life is full. And the two are deeply intertwined.

The key to longevity is not balance. Balance implies that both the personal and professional areas of your life receive equal time and attention. And that simply isn't the case.

When this happens, the effort to fight for balance only leads to frustration.

INTEGRATE, DON'T SEPARATE

My life changed when I quit trying to separate every aspect of my life and I instead started integrating them. Though there is a distinction between Gina McClain the Jesus-follower, wife, and mom and Gina McClain the ministry leader, these roles are filled by the same person: Me. And I'm not very good at dividing myself up.

I'm more successful in each of these roles when I allow myself to be present in these roles at the right times. If I were to spend Christmas day emailing volunteers and drawing up ministry goals for the next year, then I wouldn't be in a healthy place. I'd have forgotten who I am as a wife and a mom.

Yet, if I chose to ignore the phone call from the mom walking through a difficult divorce simply because it's after 5:00 p.m. and I'm with my family, I'd have forgotten who I am as a minister.

I'm not advocating for your children to live at the church, but I'm also not suggesting they should never be there outside of Sunday mornings. Some of the adventure of ministry is when

THE KEY TO LONGEVITY IS NOT BALANCE. BALANCE IMPLIES THAT BOTH THE PERSONAL AND PROFESSIONAL AREAS OF YOUR LIFE RECEIVE EQUAL TIME AND ATTENTION. AND THAT SIMPLY ISN'T THE CASE. MORE TIMES THAN NOT, ONE SIDE OF THE SCALES ARE TIPPED.

your executive pastor asks if you're aware that your 13-year-old was discovered on the roof of the church . . . Not that I know this from personal experience.

The key to maintaining a healthy rhythm in ministry is to understand the distinctions of who you are. First, you're a Jesus-follower. Your daily rhythm should reflect your passion and pursuit of Christ in your life. If you're a spouse or a parent, then energy in your daily rhythm should be invested in the relationships under your roof. Ministry will always demand more energy than we can give, but that's where the creativity begins.

FIND A HEALTHY PERSPECTIVE

The difference between "work" and "ministry" is a fine line in my home. My kids don't often know the difference. I wish I could say I've led well as our family has embraced a healthy perspective of the demands of ministry. But when Mom misses an afternoon soccer game because of a church service or skips Friday morning breakfast due to a funeral, the term "work" can have a negative tone.

Yet these are the aspects of ministry you can't predict or influence. They simply are—and you have to lead through them. So how do you maintain a healthy perspective? Here are two ideas for finding a healthy perspective:

Integrate Where You Can

Where it's possible to involve your spouse, kids, and the people you do life with, involve them. Give them a glimpse into your world. Let them bring support, perspective, and encouragement. Let them be a part of the story. Not only does it help them understand the journey you are on, it also grafts their hearts to the very thing that drives you in ministry.

Talk About Where You Can't

If you do a good job integrating where you can, the times when you can't are easier to handle. Some aspects of ministry simply require your focus and attention at times that are inconvenient. But as ministry leaders, this is what we do. Fires break out in homes at the most inconvenient times, yet a firefighter's response is always the same. Show up, address the situation, and do whatever needs to be done.

Ministry life has unpredictable rhythms that can negatively impact your family if you're not careful. In fact, I wish I had Frank Bealer's book *The Myth of Balance* much earlier in my career. The ideas shared in this book could have saved me a lot of frustration through the years. This is a book every ministry leader should have on their bookshelf.

CHECK YOUR PULSE

We all go to the doctor for an annual physical, right? #Smirk. Have you ever noticed that the doctor always checks your pulse? No matter why you see the doctor—whether you're sick or not—they take your pulse as one of the routine vitals because it's an indication of general health. If something is wrong with your pulse, additional tests will ensue.

In ministry, you need a pulse check. You need someone regularly checking to see how you're doing. When it comes to healthy integration of ministry, we all need someone outside our situation checking to see if we are healthy. Do you have that person?

This is the person that isn't afraid to speak their mind. They don't have a problem telling you when your breath stinks or when the rah-rah monologue you gave your volunteer team didn't quite hit the mark. This person is your truth-teller.

It isn't that they're negative. Actually, they're probably one of your biggest fans. And because they believe in you so much, they want to help you by helping you see things you can't see on your own.

They'll see when your focus is off. They'll notice when you're investing your identity in what you do rather than who you're becoming. So find that truth-teller in your life and set up some regular appointments to have your pulse checked.

HELP YOUR FAMILY FIND THEIR FIT

I think one of the biggest mistakes you can make in ministry is to rely on your family to meet every last-minute volunteer need you have. Avoid the trap. Sure, your family is willing to do more for you than your average volunteer. But don't abuse it. Help your family find their fit in ministry, even if it means they don't serve on your team.

Whether it's your kids, spouse, parents, or second-cousin-twice-removed, make sure you treat them like you would anyone else on your team. Your goal is to help them discover a place to serve that taps their talents, brings them joy, and connects them to the greater work God is doing in your church.

Ask yourself if your role in ministry is putting additional strain on your family. **Integrate where you can** so you build memories through shared experiences. Ministry together can be a lot of fun. **Get a pulse check** by keeping a cadence of accountability. Invite a trusted friend to ask hard questions. Listen to their guidance and don't shy away. They'll see things you might miss. You'll be grateful for their influence in the long run. And **help your family discover their ministry fit**. Your spouse and kids bring unique gifts and experiences to your church. Help them see where they fit, even if it isn't on your team.

You don't have to be in ministry for long to understand the tension of work responsibilities and quality family time. If we sat down over a cup of coffee, you'd have your own tales of crazy mishaps when ministry life and personal life collided. And after a good laugh at ourselves, my final words to you would be simple. I want you to win. I want you to wake up each day with a sense of confidence for what lies ahead. I want you to move forward with a firm assurance that your attention and energy is invested on the right things. Don't waste time chasing the unicorn of balance.

5

CHAPTER

EMBRACING LIMITATIONS

Gina McClain

I can remember the days when the only way I saw another church's ministry environments was if I traveled to visit them. These churches could be in my community or in another state—the distance didn't matter. In order for me to see their physical spaces, I had to intentionally go to them.

Now, with the magic of the "interwebs" and the emergence of social media, all I have to do is scroll through my social media feeds and I can immediately see hundreds of churches posting pictures of stage sets, wall murals, room designs, and much, much more.

Between Instagram, Facebook, *(the)* Twitter, and Pinterest, we can capture ideas from ministry leaders across the globe and use them in our own contexts to engage more people. These types of everyday connections have made my ministry better by providing new ideas and showing me what's possible. The downside is that seeing the resources other ministry leaders have at their fingertips takes the comparison game to a whole new level.

But here's the truth: No one is posting pictures of their disorganized closets for all to see. It doesn't matter what filter you choose, those aren't nearly as fun to highlight. Yet we've all experienced those moments when our spaces look like they could be featured on A&E's show *Hoarders*, our volunteer vacancies outnumber the roles we have filled, and our budget shortages have us poised for a miracle.

We all face limitations.

Most commonly, these limitations show up in the areas of

budget, space, time, and volunteers. Of course other limitations can exist, but these four categories cover the main ones the majority of ministry leaders experience.

For a season, I allowed limitations to dictate what could be accomplished in my ministry. It wasn't until a mentor challenged my thinking. He said, "If you had unlimited resources, what would you try to accomplish?" It didn't take me long to rattle off a few key objectives I wanted to see happen if I could just negotiate a larger budget, find more time, and wrangle enough volunteers.

He locked eyes with me and said, "Then why aren't you chasing after those now? You serve a God that is unlimited. It sounds to me like *you* are the limiting factor here."

That was a convicting moment. As I walked away from that conversation, I had an honest moment with myself. I asked myself *what would happen if I embraced these limitations, rather than resented them? Could this lead to a greater level of creativity and ingenuity within my ministry?*

With the remainder of this chapter, I want to show you that limitations don't have to be negative. Many times, they can be catalysts for creativity. And if you want to view your limitations through new eyes, here are just two ways you can begin to shift your perspective: by focusing on what you do have and by looking beyond yourself.

FOCUS ON WHAT YOU DO HAVE
We all have the choice to look at what we have as "not enough" or "just the beginning." If we take our cue from Scripture, there are several circumstances we can point to and see where God took a little and multiplied it. For example, look in Second Kings at the story of the prophet's widow. After the loss of her husband, she faced the potential loss of her sons to a creditor. Desperate to make ends meet, she turned to the prophet Elisha for help.

First, Elisha asked her what resources she already had. Even

LIMITATIONS DON'T HAVE TO BE NEGATIVE. MANY TIMES, THEY CAN BE CATALYSTS FOR CREATIVITY.

though she explained she only had a small jar of oil, he directed her to go and gather as many jars as she could from her neighbors. He told her not to just ask for a few, but to find as many as possible. Then his instructions were simple: "Go inside and shut the door behind you and your sons. Pour oil into all the jars, and as each is filled, put it to one side" (2 Kings 4:4 NIV). From the widow's small supply of oil, she filled every single vessel she and her sons collected. Selling these jars of oil, she was able to pay off her debts and keep her sons.

Every time I read this passage, I'm compelled by the solution Elisha offered. Elisha's focus was completely different from that of the widow. While she focused on what she *didn't* have, Elisha focused on what she *did* have.

Notice that the abundance of the miracle the widow and her sons experienced was in direct proportion to the number of jars they were willing to gather. The number of jars they were willing to gather was a reflection of their faith.

So how many jars did they gather? We don't know. But it was enough to pay off her debts and have more left over. But do you think if she had it to do over again, the widow would have figured out where to find more jars?

I'm not sure if you struggle with this, but I can easily look at my resources and view them as "not enough." The finite nature of these resources holds the potential to reveal an infinite God who isn't limited by what I have. He is limited only by the faith I have in what He can do.

Just like the small amount of oil in the widow's possession, what do you have that God could use to multiply and exceed your need?

Shortly after transitioning to a new church several years ago, I felt a little like the widow. The task before me was to prepare the ministry for a multi-site model. This took some effort, as the church had been located in a single location for more than 15 years. I'd just transitioned from Life.Church where I had the benefit of being part of the shift from single location to multi-site. I was familiar with the roadblocks, challenges, and general shifts necessary to successfully move to a multi-site model.

But the task at hand and resources available just didn't match up. It seemed like everywhere I turned, all I saw was "not enough." Not enough time to prepare, not enough volunteers to launch a campus, and not enough budget to make this happen. I couldn't get away from it.

Just like the widow, I needed to borrow from the faith of someone else in order to break out of the tailspin mindset of "not enough."

Do you find it interesting that the widow came to Elisha in the first place? Do you think she did so because she already knew of his miracles? Most likely. Her husband was one of his students. She was probably very aware of Elisha's reputation. We don't get a lot of backstory on the widow. We don't know if she sought help from others before she turned to Elisha. We don't know how long she languished in the feeling of "not enough."

But my simple take on this moment is this: If I'm in need of a miracle and looking for help, I want to turn to the most faith-filled person I know.

The difficulty with the challenges we face is we want others to validate that we do in fact have problems. We see what's happening (or not happening), and we want others to see it as a problem too. Commiseration makes us feel better.

But others validating our problem is not the solution. The solution is to stop focusing on the problem and focus on the One who can resolve it.

When I was in the middle of my "not enough" tailspin, I turned to a friend. I had several people that would sympathize with me. But I knew I needed someone who would pull me out of the rut I was in and help me see something I wasn't capable of seeing on my own.

Who do you have that can help you out of your "not enough" spiral? Who do you borrow faith from when you don't have enough faith on your own? You need these people in your life to help you see that what you have isn't a recipe for failure, but an opportunity for God to show up.

LOOK BEYOND YOURSELF
One of the dumbest things I've done in leadership is assume that when a problem arises, I'm the one responsible for bringing a solution. It sounds ridiculous when I write it down. But there was a time I really believed that because I was the one in charge, I had to be the source of every solution.

Unrealistic expectations paired with a fear of failure make for a disastrous combination, a dumpster fire waiting to happen.

As you lead, you will discover that some of the limitations you face are not external. They're internal. Sometimes limitations have more to do with your weaknesses—things you're simply not good at.

I've had to grow ridiculously comfortable with the fact that I'm not good with details. It's not that I don't care. It's just that I seriously don't see them!

I remember talking to a team member one day before flying out of town.

She asked, "What time does your flight leave?"

I responded, "I don't know."

"What airline are you flying?"

"I haven't checked yet."

"You seriously don't know what airline you're flying!?"

I wasn't quite sure what the problem was. We were hours away from my departure. I knew I had the info in a file that I could refer to the moment I needed it. And "that moment" hadn't arrived yet.

I'm not justifying my crazy thinking. I'm just saying I'd prefer not to clutter up my thought process with details.

This ability serves me well when it comes to leading because I am good at seeing the big picture and recognizing how things work together to achieve the greater goal. But if I'm not careful, my inability to manage details can be a liability.

Knowing my strength doesn't lie in the realm of logistics, I have to rely heavily on those that do. It means I have to remain committed to hearing and heeding their input as I lead the ministry. If I refuse to listen, it's to the detriment of the ministry I lead.

It's so important to understand where you bring strength and where you might create a problem. When you embrace your weaknesses, you're better prepared to lean on those whose strengths can counteract them. You're better equipped to call greatness out of those around you.

Isn't this ultimately what we're called to do? Isn't our purpose in leadership to draw the best out of others? Go ahead, embrace your limitations. When you own your weaknesses, you will create opportunities for others to show off their strengths.

6

CHAPTER

CLARIFYING
THE WIN

Gina McClain

Having grown up in Oklahoma, I'm accustomed to tornado season. Every time the seasons change in that part of the country, the weather conditions are ripe for straight-line winds, lots of rain, and funnel clouds that drop out of the sky and sweep everything into chaos.

Sitting in a local coffee shop recently, I was spending time with a key volunteer. She was relatively new to her leadership role and hungry to learn more. After reading through some books published by Orange, she had one important question for me.

"Gina, what **is** the win?"

She wanted to know, out of all the things we do as a ministry to create a great experience for kids to connect and as a church to go into our community to reach those who are far from God, what's the main point.

For years, when I was asked questions like that one, a tornado of thoughts would blow through my mind. I would open my mouth and all that would come out was a funnel cloud full of ideas and perspectives that sounded good but ultimately created a path of chaos and confusion.

In my ministry, we've accomplished so many things. From creating preschool environments that are warm and inviting to establishing elementary environments that are fun and engaging. From local mission events that send families into their communities to serve to a weekly discipleship ministry that creatively leads kids to dig deeper into Scripture. There are so many things to point to and say, "This is the win!"

But actually, if everything disappeared overnight and all I had left was one small group leader, a child, and the child's parent, my response to that question would be very simple.

I would say the win happens when a small group leader successfully connects with a kid or student and finds a way to cue the parent.

I want to create a culture in which the scoreboard reflects the number of times we do exactly that. It really can be that simple. And that simplicity transcends all other challenges you might face.

Whether your budget is big or small, your facility is brand-new or old, your staff is expansive or you're flying solo, the win can be the straightforward objective to connect kids and students to community and cue parents for conversation.

If, like me and my church, this is your main objective, then you should know there are great tools out there to help you do this even better. Orange is constantly releasing new resources as part of their Phase Project and Parent Cue strategies. They've been a go-to resource for myself and countless other ministry leaders, and I think you'll love how they come alongside leaders like you in supporting families.

CHECK YOUR POSTURE
I remember a conversation I had with a small group leader over a year ago. Sitting in front of a Dunkin Donuts on a warm summer morning, I was sipping a fresh cup of coffee while listening to the experiences of this young teacher working in an under-resourced school in our community.

At one point in the conversation, I said, "Jenna, one of the driving perspectives in our ministry is that we believe every parent wants to be a better parent." With conviction, she locked eyes with me and said, "I don't believe that's true."

Her experiences teaching in her school told her a different story and shaped her perspective in a different way. She existed in an environment where the majority of kids go home every Friday with a backpack full of food more likely to be eaten by someone else, and where the concern around exposure to drugs isn't in the neighborhood playgrounds, but in the child's living room.

Her experience told her that parents don't really want to be better parents. It actually seemed to her as though they didn't want to be parents at all. What she learned to expect from parents was a lack of desire for any level of engagement with their child.

These are harsh realities that shaped one of my best volunteer's perspectives. I bet the same is true of some of your volunteers as well. Their experiences with parents in the past have shaped what they expect in the future.

As a leader, you are working to shape (or reshape) the perspectives of the volunteers you lead. Reshaping these perspectives makes the difference between your volunteers adopting or rejecting the postures that shape your ministry wins.

Clarifying the win in your ministry begins with identifying the foundational postures that define why you do what you do. At Faith Promise Church, there are a few postures we won't be swayed from:

1. We believe people are created for community. Everyone is hardwired to live and grow in relationship with God and other people.
2. We believe faith grows in the context of healthy community. Our ministry exists to provide healthy community for kids to grow in their faith.
3. We believe every parent wants to be a better parent. They are looking for ways to engage their kids meaningfully.

Establishing these postures equips us to determine where to focus our resources first.

DEFINE YOUR FOCUS
Focus is a discipline.

The willingness to say no to good things so you can say yes to the best things requires a remarkable amount of discipline. But this level of focus is rare. Few leaders choose it. Why? Because it's hard to obtain and even more difficult to keep.

Focus means you prioritize values. You choose to build your volunteer team in layers. You intentionally focus on building your volunteer team around the most impactful roles. That might mean you predominantly use curriculum-based videos as the element for your main teaching rather than live storytelling or skits, so you can funnel your volunteer resources toward establishing a strong team of small group leaders.

In my ministry, focus means identifying specific behaviors or opportunities to create healthy community for kids and cue parents for faith conversations. I have to pinpoint where we have the greatest chance of accomplishing those two things.

That unrelenting focus is the lens through which you view your strategy.

EXAMINE YOUR STRATEGY
Every action you take, every event you host, and every procedure you have in place is your strategy in action. If your strategy is not moving you closer to your goal, then the strategy is not working.

As one of many leaders in your church, you may not have veto power over events or programming within the ministry you lead. The question is, can you influence these events or programs so they produce better outcomes? Can you focus the outcomes of these events or programs to move you closer to your win statement?

I lead in a context where I have two competing values. We offer multiple worship service times in order to maximize the amount of space we have in our building. Adding services is one of the most cost effective ways to increase capacity without adding square footage to your building. As a result we have multiple service times that accommodate busy families. Sports schedules, travel plans, and trips to the local amusement park can crowd out the time families have on the weekend. A variety of time options to attend church allow those families to find a time that fits their schedule for that weekend.

Yet the value of offering multiple time options to fill our worship center as many times as possible can compete with the value of creating consistent small groups for kids. Our small group programming for kids is incorporated into our weekend worship services so we can provide the small group experience at the time families are most likely to show up at church—during the weekend worship service. However, the culture of "come when you can" creates inconsistency within our small groups. A child may come to church every week and yet **when** they come could vary from one weekend to the next. The value for options can compete with our value for consistency.

I'm not in a position to influence the number of worship services we offer at our church. But I am in a position to influence the way the programming works during those worship services.

I can't decide to cut a few worship services so families only have one or two choices. But I can orchestrate a system that creates the highest level of consistency possible within the framework I have to work in.

Examining your strategy means you view everything you do by asking the question, "Does this move me closer to my goal?" In other words, does this support the foundational postures your ministry is rooted in? If it doesn't, are you willing to break it? Sometimes you have to break something that's working to discover how it can work better.

A few years ago, we made the difficult decision to elevate small groups above everything else in our ministry. We did this because we believe small groups are the most strategic way to accomplish our goal. That meant every system, every support,

and every process we had must support the small group model.
If it didn't, we broke it and started over.

The process of examining our strategy and making the necessary
changes was the hardest thing we've had to do. But the payoff
has been immeasurable.

BEAT THAT DRUM

I spent my high school career in the marching band. One year
we were a featured band in the annual Fiesta Bowl Parade.
Marching in a parade while playing an instrument isn't as easy
as it might appear. When it comes to marching and playing
music, the most important instrument in the lineup is the bass
drum.

The bass drum keeps the beat. If the bass is off, the entire band
falls out-of-sync. In a parade that lasts five miles, if the bass
drummer decides to have a bad day, the ripple effect can be
comical.

When it comes to clarifying the win, you are the bass drum. You
are the most important instrument in the lineup because you
keep all the other instruments playing to the same beat.

Beating the drum is critical. Without it, all the work you've done
to this point may never get off the ground. Or worse, it will get
off the ground only to unravel over time.

Once you've checked your posture, defined your focus, and
examined your strategy, you get to beat the drum. You get to be
the biggest champion of your strategy. You get to show people
over and over again what a win looks like. You get to set the beat
to which your volunteer team walks.

As you do this, you'll discover key volunteers who will join
you in keeping the rhythm. You can leverage their influence to
increase the volume of the beat. As the beat gets louder, even
more people will fall in line with the music.

The key to beating the drum is summarizing the most important

YOU GET TO BE THE
BIGGEST CHAMPION
OF YOUR STRATEGY.
YOU GET TO SHOW
PEOPLE OVER AND
OVER AGAIN WHAT
A WIN LOOKS LIKE.
YOU GET TO SET
THE BEAT TO WHICH
YOUR VOLUNTEER
TEAM WALKS.

thing your ministry does and repeating it over and over and over again. You may get tired of saying it, but that's just about the time everyone else will begin hearing it.

That day, sitting across from that key volunteer - the one in the new leadership role - I had an opportunity to clarify the win for her. As she slid the book I'd given her back across the table, she asked, "Gina, what **is** the win?"

I said, "It's engaging the child in a consistent small group where they can have a conversation about faith, and cueing the parent to continue the conversation. Every time we do this, it's another point on the scoreboard."

The win might not always come easily. It will require laser focus and a defined strategy. More than anything, it will take a leader ready to act as the bass drum, keeping the entire band in rhythm, moving in the same direction. That leader is you.

7

CHAPTER

THE
THREE Cs
OF HEALTHY
CONFLICT

Jessica Bealer

A healthy team experiences conflict. If you can't remember the last time you had an impassioned disagreement with someone you work alongside, your organization or ministry is probably not as healthy as it seems. Passionate people advocate fiercely for what they believe. If disputes rarely arise, I might question if you really care or if a fear of displacement or relational disillusionment supersedes the calling on your life. That may sound harsh, but we're talking about *conflict*. What would be the point of this chapter if it didn't challenge your current model of conflict resolution . . . or the lack thereof.

Conflict is uncomfortable for everyone. When personalities or opinions are at odds, tension is created. Don't let the experts fool you, tension creates anxiety no matter how well you learn to manage it. Why is this? Why is it so difficult to address our innate differences? Logically, we all know we are designed by God to be unique individuals, and raised in varied households with drastically different outlooks on life. It's to be expected that our mindsets may not always align. Yet, this knowledge doesn't seem to motivate most of us to address the differences we have with those with whom we don't see eye-to-eye.

After nearly a decade of avoiding conflict in my own ministry, I distinctly remember sitting down at my desk one morning with a multitude of problems that needed to be solved, but having no clue where to start. I felt like one of those crazy stunt men who lock themselves into a crate that's then thrown into dark, watery depths. I was drowning. My ministry was sinking and, to make matters worse, I had handcuffed myself with the idea that I should avoid upsetting anyone at anytime. I was afraid to make a call that might not sit well with everyone on my team. I was terrified of talking with a volunteer whose attitude seemed to drag down morale. I was worried about how I would be perceived if I lobbied for a portion of the budget to be reallocated to my ministry. I was scared of seemingly nothing.

The unknown can be paralyzing. It plays out in our minds a dozen different ways, each scene worse than the last. It was around that ten-year mark in ministry that I heard a fellow leader say, "Play it out. What's the worst-case scenario? Wrap your mind around that. Decide a course of action if it were to actually come true, and press onward." It was a simple, but incredibly liberating idea. It also empowered me to prepare for the worst, but hope for the best. Either way, I was ready.

Here's an example of how this helped me. At the time, there was a volunteer leader that consistently undermined my authority. She would ask me a question. I would give her an answer. She would then go do whatever she wanted, with little regard to the direction I gave. I spent far too much time undoing what she had done, and cleaning up the collateral damage of a divided leadership front.

However, when it came to confronting this volunteer, there was a continuous loop of what-ifs in my head, "What if she starts yelling? What if she leaves? What if she causes other people to leave? What if she goes to my supervisor and makes up a lie that causes me to lose my job?" Okay, that last one was a little over the top, but you get the idea. The likelihood that I would lose my job because I addressed my concerns with one volunteer was very unlikely. However, if it was a possibility in my mind, I ran with it and played it out to the worst possible conclusion. When I did this, I came to the stark realization that the worst-case scenario was acceptable. I didn't want to lose my job, but if I did because I had not gained the trust of my senior leadership, then it was possible I needed to move on anyway. Once I understood the "play it out" principle, it relieved me of my fear.

Those early days of learning healthy conflict resolution were not easy ones. I wasn't a master by any means. Over time,

JUST AS A ROAD
TRIP IS LESS
PROBLEMATIC
WITH NAVIGATION,
CONFLICT IS MORE
EASILY TRAVERSED
WHEN YOU HAVE
A PLAN AND A
DESTINATION.

confrontation became less terrifying and more practical. One of the best ways I've found to prepare for the awkward conversations we all must endure is to make a plan. When you know where you're going and why you're going there, it reduces anxiety. Have you ever climbed in your car, aware of your destination, but only vaguely remembered how to get there? I've done this more times than I can count. One of my kids will say, "Mom, do you know where you're going?" I'll respond with, "I think so." For the next few minutes my stress level is off the charts as I hope I don't get lost. It's ridiculous. Every smartphone in America has a GPS app on it, yet there I am driving in circles, getting no closer to my destination, because I'm too stubborn to take the time to type in the address.

Just as a road trip is less problematic with navigation, conflict is more easily traversed when you have a plan and a destination. Using the example of a small group leader who consistently fails to prepare for their lesson before the weekend, here are three steps—what I call the three Cs—to help you navigate your next tough conversation.

COMPLIMENT

Start with a personal compliment. Find a character trait, a skill set, or a good deed that can be praised. Be honest. The truth is, just because you need to confront someone doesn't mean they have bad intentions. So search your heart and find a complimentary way to bridge the conversation.

Example: "I love the way you interact with the kids in your small group. You take the time to connect with each child, and make them feel special."

CRITIQUE

This is the most difficult part of any confrontation. Be specific. Don't get distracted with too much detail, but address the problem head on. Avoid using words like "always" or "never." Don't accuse. Instead think of this as a chance to reveal another point of view. Often times, your volunteers just need guidance. When done right, a well-handled confrontation might not even communicate a hint of conflict.

Example: "I noticed that while you were connecting with the kids, it didn't seem as if you were well prepared to work through the activities in the lesson plan."

CONSTRUCT

The point of all conflict is to grow and mature both parties. Offering a critique can be helpful, but only if it's paired with vision and direction. Remember where you want to go and what result you're trying to build toward.

Example: "Because you hold the attention of the kids in your group so well, I really feel they would listen and participate even better if you were to spend more time preparing your lesson. I can help you if you'd like."

If your motives are pure, and you truly want what's best for both the individual and the ministry, conflict will be a healthy catalyst for necessary change—in both parties. Your next level of ministry may be one confrontational conversation away. Conflict isn't a bad thing. It's the way we press into and challenge one another to pursue excellence with a heart fully focused on the mission God has called each of us to.

CONFLICT PITFALLS TO AVOID

- Avoiding avoidance.

- Talking to the wrong person—meaning anyone other than the individual—about the problem.

- Assuming ill intent. It builds on the problem and makes it bigger in your mind.

- Choosing to be offended before you've approached the individual.

- Subverting the authority of the Bible by having someone else "handle" it.

- Making an overarching rule with underlying motives.

8

CHAPTER

PLAYING WELL
WITH OTHERS

Gina McClain

There was a time when I was convinced that if the ministry I led was successful, I'd done my job. In fact, not only did I think I'd done my job, I also believed leadership should celebrate me. Because when I stopped to look around, the ministry leaders I served beside were not nearly as successful as me! I'm not sure what their problem was. And if they'd ever asked, I would have been happy to help.

In all honesty, when my coworkers experienced wins in their ministries, I was happy for them. I would cheer them on and celebrate what they'd accomplished. Unless, of course, they were more successful than me—then I wasn't nearly as excited. I mean, I was perfectly fine if those around me had *some* wins, as long as I stayed ahead of them.

My competitive nature can be one of my strengths, but in this season, it was out of check. It had grown into a monstrous liability that, if left unaddressed, would have taken me out of ministry. I had a myopic perspective when it came to the ministry I led. And I had no idea the damage I was doing to the student pastor and other ministry leaders I served alongside.

The ministry you lead is part of a larger whole. Your church has a purpose in your community. So if your ministry is moving toward that purpose, yet the other ministries in your church are not, that's not a win. That's an indicator that something is missing.

I have these childhood memories of playing soccer with my classmates. Soccer was a big deal but it was always a gamble whether or not we would get to play. It wasn't a lack of willingness on our part. We usually already had our teams picked before lunch was over. Whether or not we played soccer was always determined by whether or not we had a ball.

Balls on the playground were scarce. If there was one, it was snatched up quickly for a game of kickball, basketball, soccer, or any other games our minds could create.

With so many kids and so few balls, getting our hands on one was the highest priority. When the bell rang for recess it was a dead sprint to make it to the ball bin if you wanted half a chance at playing.

Some kids figured out that having a ball made them a favored player. If they were the first to the ball bin, they would leverage their possession and bargain their way to their favorite spot on the team. It took a pretty generous person to be willing to give up a ball without any conditions attached.

My elementary school playground was one big social experiment. Learning to share opportunities, compromise, and really celebrate when someone else scored a point. It's no wonder behavioral scientists point to playground dynamics as great way to learn social skills.

When I sit in staff meetings with my peers, it's not hard to remember the days on the playground. The battles over equipment and games closely mimic our present day conversations about volunteers, budget, and space. It's a constant tension.

A tension in which . . .

- resources are tight and winning the "ball" for your ministry means another ministry might not get to play.
- wins reflect success and you're only willing to cheer on another ministry when their win doesn't outshine yours.
- strategies collide because you believe winning requires aggressive offense while another peer believes in dominant defense.

Learning to support the ministry leaders and teams around you is an important skill that your senior leadership needs from you. And to do this well, you have to actively make three critical choices.

CHOOSE TO SEE THE BIGGER PICTURE

You have a passion for your ministry. It's why you're leading it. Your drive for kids or students to encounter Jesus runs high and you have lots of ideas about how to create environments where kids and students can grow in their faith.

Yet it's critical to remember that your ministry is just one piece of a larger whole. For example, it could be that when you're given additional budget dollars for a project or event, another ministry team might be denied the same opportunity.

The reality of shared resources is something all of us can identify with on some level. There are only so many volunteers, budget dollars, square feet, and hours to go around. Budget planning can feel a little like the foot race to the ball bin on the playground. You want to be the first one there so you can get your hands on what you need to stay in the game.

All of these resources have to be allocated to ministry areas based upon vision, values, and availability. And you make yourself a great asset to your senior leadership when you can appreciate the challenge it can be to allocate these resources.

Your role at your church is to pursue the resources necessary so your ministry can help advance the vision of your church. But it can't be to the detriment of other ministry teams. Sometimes the right move is to hand the ball to another leader and let them run with it for a while.

CHOOSE TO CELEBRATE OTHERS

Do you celebrate other ministry leaders in your church?

I mean, do you *really* celebrate them? That can be a hard question to answer.

SOMETIMES THE
RIGHT MOVE IS TO
HAND THE BALL TO
ANOTHER LEADER
AND LET THEM
RUN WITH IT FOR
A WHILE.

As an elementary kid on the school playground, my competitive nature often got the best of me. When another kid on the team was a better player than me, I took it personally. It made me want to work harder so others would see that I could be just as good.

There's an internal drive there that has served me well as an adult. But left unchecked, it could become a real hindrance. To be honest, my intensely competitive nature has definitely gotten in the way in the past. The truth is, I find it easier to celebrate the success of my peers as long as their success doesn't outshine mine.

Several years ago, I found myself at a real growth opportunity when another ministry was experiencing greater success and momentum than mine. In my head I knew I should be excited. I should be cheering. I should be celebrating with them. But deep in my heart, there was a battle going on. Why wasn't I experiencing the same momentum? Why were they making breakthroughs and finding success when I felt like I was barely surviving?

Because I fostered such a selfish perspective in my heart I couldn't see what God was doing in my church. And it hindered me from really celebrating those around me.

Our peers are not our competitors. They are our *teammates*. And a healthy teammate lets others shine.

CHOOSE TO PUBLICLY SUPPORT AND PRIVATELY CONFRONT
Your ability to play well with others hinges on your ability to publicly support and privately confront. In fact, I would suggest that the extent to which you privately confront directly affects how well you publicly support.

This concept is so simple. When you have a conflict with a peer, you privately confront them. You let them know what you see, how you feel, and what you need from them. You enter the conversation with a humble and teachable spirit. You engage in open, honest dialogue to bring resolution to the problem. And when you walk away from that conversation, you agree on who will do what and by when.

But no matter how well the conversation goes—whether you come to a resolution or simply agree to disagree—once you walk away from that conversation, you choose to honor that leader publicly. Period.

There's no exception to this rule.

Any challenges you might face with another ministry leader in your church should not be public knowledge. In fact, it should shock someone to know there is even a disagreement. Playing well with others begins with honoring them enough to bring your disagreements directly to them and engaging in open, honest dialogue. There's no integrity in a leader who airs their grievances with those who are not part of the solution. Don't be that leader.

If you find yourself reading this and realizing this is a problem for you, then make a commitment to address the issue right now. Prioritize it on your to-do list. Schedule time with the ministry leader with whom you're in conflict. Write down the grievances you have. Enter that meeting with an open and humble heart. Truly share where you're at and what you need. Be prepared to listen . . . really listen. Invite the person to meet on an ongoing basis to continue the conversation and keep the lines of communication open.

Don't fall prey to the belief that you can keep your grievances hidden. Like weeds in a flowerbed, they'll pop up everywhere. You can't control it. Your senior leadership needs assurance that you are willing to fight for the team. And fighting for the team means having the humility to honor others by privately confronting the problem, so you can publicly support the individual.

FIGHTING FOR THE TEAM MEANS HAVING THE HUMILITY TO HONOR OTHERS BY PRIVATELY CONFRONTING THE PROBLEM, SO YOU CAN PUBLICLY SUPPORT THE INDIVIDUAL.

9

CHAPTER

CREATING UNITY THROUGH A COMMON LANGUAGE

Jessica Bealer

L et's start this chapter with a fun exercise. Look at these slogans and see how quickly you can identify the company to which they belong.

Just Do It™
Melts in Your Mouth, Not in Your Hand™
America Runs on _____.™
I'm Lovin' It.™
Can You Hear Me Now? Good.™
Like a Good Neighbor, _____ _____ *Is There.*™
Maybe She's Born With It. Maybe It's _____.™
The Few. The Proud. The _____.™
The Quicker Picker-Upper™
There are some things money can't buy. For everything else, there's _____.™

How did you do? I suspect you got an A. In the business world, a slogan can become as strong an identifier as the company itself. The purpose of a slogan is to audibly represent the brand. The goal for any advertising companies is to build brand awareness and impart positive feelings towards that brand.

I know you're probably wondering what's up with the marketing lesson. In the book *It's Just a Phase*, Reggie Joiner and Kristen Ivy explain just how important clear communication is: "Over time, words create a common language to keep everyone motivated and aligned. But words should be more than inspiring. They should also be insightful and strategic."

Being strategic means you know the goal of the language you will be creating before you actually start constructing it. It begins by asking yourself, "What words or phrases identify my ministry? How can I combine those in a memorable way that will represent the vision and bring inspiration?"

At Elevation Church, there was something we called the "One Day Principle." It was taught in volunteer orientation classes and reinforced regularly in team meetings. The idea behind the "One Day Principle" was simple. In every worship experience, there are specific individuals God intends to speak to and move in their hearts in a mighty way. Maybe their family has prayed for them. Maybe coworkers have invited them a dozen times. Maybe at some point, their life fell apart, along with their faith, and now something is missing. And that moment, that *day*, may be their one chance to come back to Jesus.

As a volunteer, what would you do to facilitate that encounter? Would you smile bigger as they parked their car? Would your encounter at the door be welcoming or routine? Would you walk their children to their classrooms or simply point down the hall? Would you find them a great seat or just tell them where the auditorium is? Would you do everything possible to limit distractions during the worship experience or just pray the batteries don't go out in the microphone again? The "One Day Principle" is inspirational, memorable, and it differentiates a committed volunteer from an average attendee. It conveys a clear expectation of excellence and personal connection, both of which are priorities of the church.

Creating a common language that both conveys your values and unites your team is deceivingly hard. To be memorable, it has to be clear, easy to say, founded in vision, purposeful, and have a touch of cleverness. Getting your teams to memorize or prioritize language is a difficult task all by itself, but without creativity and an objective, it's futile. However, with a little intentionality, you can use language to reinforce your values and unite your teams in a common goal.

There are a few keys to creating a common language that marry purpose with inspiration. Here are a few ideas to get you started.

IDENTIFY WHAT'S IMPORTANT

There are a lot of things that need to be done in your ministry, but not everything is deserving of distinctive language. For a word, phrase, or vision statement to have staying power it must speak to the heart of who you are as an organization.

For example, although I value cleanliness, I wouldn't put language around it. Is it important for those I lead to clean up after themselves? Yes. Is it one of the most important things we do? No.

A quick way to identify your highest priorities is to ask yourself, "As a ministry, if we could only do three things from this point forward, what would they be?" Here is how I would answer that question:

1. Engage kids with God's Word.
2. Empower parents to grow their child's faith.
3. Create a fun and safe environment where every family feels welcome.

GET CREATIVE

The slogans at the beginning of this chapter are anything but mundane. They are fresh, innovative, and bring clarity to their brands. The language you create should immediately speak to the heart of your organization. It should define you in a word or phrase and it should be catchy. Catchy doesn't mean weird. Don't try to create words—stick to those in the dictionary. But don't be afraid to push past the words you've always associated with your ministry and try something different. In eKidz, we created a question for volunteers to use to check their intentionality with parents. We would ask, *"What WOW moments have you created today?"* What we were really asking was, "How have you gone above and beyond to connect with a family today to the level that a parent would say, 'Wow, they really love and care for us!'" It was a simple turn of phrase, but it gave memorable, easy to understand language to a ministry priority.

ASK FOR INPUT

One of the best ways to generate buy-in is to request input before you implement. Your teams are far more likely to get on board if they understand the purpose behind key words and phrases and feel as though they were part of the creative process. When you allow committed leaders to weigh in and take ownership, you'll see the words you're attempting to disseminate begin to grow and develop organically. Over time, the common language of your team will actually transform into insider language. And is there anything better than an old story shared among long-time friends, or the feeling that comes when you collaborate with others who just "get it"? Ask for input and you'll get more than just suggestions, you'll get *unity*.

USE IT CONSISTENTLY

It can feel awkward at first when you've named something or put language around a priority, but the easiest way to discount the new language you've created is to neglect to use it. For years I led a meeting entitled "BP." The letters stood for two things: Blood Pressure and Best Practices. The point of the meeting was for me to assess the health (Blood Pressure) of our many campuses and for Campus Directors to gain insight into what's working on other campuses (Best Practices). When we first named the meeting it sounded weird to say, "Will you be in BP?" Honestly, that sounds like the beginning of bad potty humor, but the language stuck and the leaders involved each week knew what the two letters stood for. Four years later, the letters BP are as clearly understood as our Ministry Values.

The point here is that you have to sell out to the language you create. If you're going to name something, then call it by that name. My parents call me "Jessica," not "that blonde girl who goes by our last name." Don't undermine your efforts with forgetfulness, carelessness, or fear of awkwardness. Keep in mind, there's going to be an incubation period with newly introduced language, and the best way for you to nurture it is to stay pure to the intent and use it as often as possible.

CHANGE IT . . . BUT DO SO INFREQUENTLY

When I described the "One Day Principle" at the beginning of this chapter, you may have noticed I said we taught the concept

THINK OF YOUR LANGUAGE AS A SECRET HANDSHAKE TO THE GREATEST CLUB EVER CREATED. WHEN YOU GET THIS RIGHT, IT WILL DEEPEN COMMITMENT AND SUPPORT UNITY AMONG YOUR TEAM.

for years in our volunteer orientation meetings. That doesn't mean it's still taught today. Over time language can become so habitually used it becomes watered down or the meaning gets distorted by generational misconception. If a phrase or terminology doesn't inspire action or bring clarity, it's time for new language. The "One Day Principle," while still absolutely true, now earns a brief mention where before it garnered a 15-minute explanation. Replace language when it becomes antiquated or commonplace, but don't change it too often. The key is to watch for that moment when inspiration has become convention and choose to make a bittersweet retirement.

All the members of your team have a unique set of circumstances that brought them to where they are today. Their upbringing has molded them. Their relationships have influenced them. Their career choices, in many ways, may define them. With such diversity, it may seem impossible to find shared commonality. However, each of them has a starring role in God's grand story. Each of them exists to make the name of Jesus famous. And while they may not realize it, each of them yearns to realize a greater purpose in Christ. They wouldn't have signed up to volunteer if they didn't. Use this knowledge to build camaraderie. Think of your language as a secret handshake to the greatest club ever created. When you get this right, it will deepen commitment and support unity among your team.

10

CHAPTER

TRAINING
VS. COACHING

Jessica Bealer

O
ur new temporary location had been open for nine weeks. As the Children's Director of the church, I had spent the first month after launch identifying and training new staff, establishing what I perceived to be healthy teams, and reviewing standards and systems.

After that first month, feeling pretty confident in the new leaders' abilities to run the campus without my constant oversight, I stepped away to allow them to fully embrace their leadership positions. I spent the next five weekends traveling to other campuses, troubleshooting problems, working with eKidz Directors to streamline systems, and showing appreciation to teams that were executing well.

On week nine, I decided it was time to go back and check on our newly launched location. At first glance, everything seemed to be functioning exactly as I had left it. The campus was beautiful, volunteers were engaged, and families seemed excited.

I remember thinking, "I may not actually need to stay here all day. This place looks great. I'll go scope out the next launch site before heading home." It was about that time that a high-level leader walked by. I smiled, put my arm around her shoulders and said, "Hey girl, it looks great! How's it been going?"

She smirked and said, "Well, it's going . . . just not sure if it's going to heaven or, you know, the other place." I was taken aback. What had happened over the last month? She then muttered one word, "Clubhouse."

Clubhouse is the area that cares for volunteer and staff kids who are on campus for more than one worship experience because their parents are serving during multiple services. It's a fun, relaxed environment where kids can watch movies, play games, hang out with friends, and eat snacks. Clubhouse is a programming dream come true because, well, *there is no programming*. As far as execution goes, it's easy.

It's funny now. It wasn't so funny when I was standing in the doorway of that classroom looking at a very broken version of what I'd left just a few weeks earlier. I remember thinking, "Where did I go wrong? I thought I had effectively communicated the systems that had to be maintained in order to provide volunteer kids with a safe, fun, and nurturing environment. What happened?"

As I peeked around the door frame, here's what I saw: The security officer assigned to Clubhouse was lying prostrate on his stomach, fierce concentration on his face as he endeavored to defeat a group of elementary-age boys in an intense game of Phase 10.

Young girls were precariously balanced against the wall in an attempt to compare their handstand techniques. The classroom desks that were supposed to be moved to the walls during Clubhouse were in their original placement and covered in assorted fragments of chicken nuggets and oozy droplets of ketchup. And the storage container we used for supplies was overflowing with trash.

Clearly, I had missed the mark with my communication. I took control of the situation, disbanded the handstand brigade, reintroduced the security officer to his post at the door, and began to clean up the mess. At the end of the experience, I met with the two young volunteers I had charged in my absence. My only question, "What happened?," was met with confused stares. One of them spoke up, "I don't know what you mean. We did exactly what you said." She then proceeded to repeat word for word what I had said.

"Security needs to be present in the room. We don't want him to scare the kids, so he needs to be engaged."

"We want the kids to love Clubhouse. We want to create a fun environment where they can hang out and do fun stuff with their friends."

"We are using a teacher's workspace. If we want to continue to have access to this room, we need to make sure it is put back together exactly as we found it."

"Because this is a non-permanent location, we can't leave anything behind. Everything has to go into the storage cart."

My mistake was blaringly obvious. I had provided the information without the intention, the details without the driving force. Empowerment starts with clarity of vision. There was nothing inherently wrong with the direction I gave to the Clubhouse volunteers. I just didn't start in the right place. If I had it to do all over again, I would have started with the purpose of Clubhouse, why it's necessary, and how it helps our entire church successfully minister to families. I would have described the look and feel of a healthy Clubhouse environment, and I would have reinforced our ministry values and explained how they affect our Clubhouse strategy.

Training is important. Volunteers have to know the systems, standards, and boundaries from which they operate. Yet of equal importance is the need for consistent coaching—a leader to remind them of the mission, keeping purpose and vision in the forefront.

TRAINING LOOKS LIKE THIS:
"We need to vacuum the carpet between services so the room stays clean."

COACHING LOOKS LIKE THIS:
"We want to provide a safe, nurturing, and sanitary environment so every parent feels comfortable leaving their child with us. Vacuuming is one of the ways we accomplish this."

In the children's ministry at Elevation Church there are more than 2,200 volunteers across many locations. For the first

EMPOWERMENT STARTS WITH CLARITY OF VISION.

few years of ministry, we attempted to keep our teams aligned through training events. Once or twice a quarter we would bring different teams from multiple locations together and review policies and procedures. Throw in a dash of vision and a pinch of purpose and what we came up with was a very ineffective training method. "Why?," you might ask. Because only about 40 percent of our volunteer base attended these training nights, and it was always the 40 percent that didn't really need the training. Essentially, we were preaching to the choir.

After many expensive and futile training events, we thought there had to be a better way. I remember sitting around a conference table with my team and asking the question, "What if we completely eradicated training events? What would we do instead?" After hours of debates and many tense conversations, we landed on an idea: coaching.

It took six months and lots of vision casting, but we were able to convince our teams to give coaching a try. Our new model would eliminate training events and focus solely on hands-on, in-the-moment feedback for both new and existing volunteers.

Volunteers were no longer required to give up another night of their week, or to discern how to apply what was being taught at those events to their weekly volunteer roles. Instead they had a seasoned leader to walk alongside them, help them work through difficulties and challenge them to strive for the next level of leadership.

When a volunteer understands his or her role, when they have a clear purpose and vision for the ministry in which they serve, and when they feel supported and encouraged, they begin to take ownership of that ministry. "They" becomes "we." "That classroom" becomes "my classroom." "Those families" becomes "my families."

Training is about how a volunteer does what they do. Coaching shapes the heart behind it. If you're ready to implement the coaching model in your ministry, keep reading. We'll dive into that in the next chapter.

11

CHAPTER

IMPLEMENTING A COACHING MODEL

Jessica Bealer

You've probably heard of the leadership principle, *renters vs. owners*. Renters care only to the point that it affects them. Owners look beyond the here and now. They plan for the future and make decisions based on investment, not preference.[1]

A coaching model produces owners by eliminating the notion of renting. A great Coach offers real-time, experienced perspective while allowing the volunteer to add in his or her own thoughts and opinions. A Coach asks the right questions and never tries to tackle more than one concern at a time, understanding how that might be detrimental to a volunteer's confidence.

Have I sold you on the coaching model yet? If so, here are a few steps to help you get started:

1. **Identify Coaches by assessing your top leaders in each ministry area**. These individuals need to clearly understand your church's vision and your ministry's purpose, and be able to plainly communicate these ideas to others. They also need to be a positive person that shows discipline.

2. **Remove your Coaches from your current organizational chart**. Assigning weekly responsibilities beyond the care and accountability of the volunteers they are coaching relays to your Coaches that mentoring is a secondary responsibility. When prioritizing one's to-do list,

---

1   You can read more about owning vs. renting in a companion book called, "Not Normal," by Sue Miller and Adam Duckworth www.NotNormalBook.com.

the urgent always replaces the essential, so take away duties that may cause distraction.

3. **Clearly outline a Coach's responsibilities, timeline, and steps with each new or existing volunteer they're advising.** Most of your Coaches will be highly disciplined and will value structure. Clear instruction will cement their dedication to the role.

4. **Encourage Coaches to document progress.** There are many ways to do this. You could have them fill out an information card or an online survey for each volunteer they coach. Either way, this encourages Coaches to celebrate the impact they are having and it allows you to monitor their effectiveness.

5. **Schedule quarterly gatherings with your Coaches and other insiders.** The mission of your church probably doesn't change often, but the strategy may change yearly, monthly, or even weekly. What worked last year may not be effective in the future. What was popular this week may fall flat next month. As your ministry strategy changes, you must keep your Coaches informed. Consider your Coaches to be insiders—those volunteers you expect to spread vision to the rest of the team. For instance, if you want to change the first-time guest experience, you need to inform your Coaches about this change as soon as possible.

An additional benefit of quarterly gatherings is they give you an opportunity to evaluate your Coaches' spiritual and emotional health.

Coaching isn't a catch-all for every problem that might come up. However, I've found that proactively pursuing excellence is more effective than reactively scheduling training nights in which you make overarching policies with underlying motives. Throwing a rule at a problem rarely produces the effect you intended. Having a clear and present strategy to address problems as they arise sets a precedent of preparedness.

I've personally seen the impact of empowerment through coaching, but it's still a fairly new concept for me as well. Several years back, in my first year of ministry at Elevation, I experienced quite the opposite. When my husband, Frank, and I first came on staff we were charged with launching a new non-permanent location within a six-week time frame. It was a whirlwind of marketing, team building, and supplies ordering. It was an experience I will never forget.

That first week, as I walked the halls of the school we had transformed into a new Elevation location, I prayed for the families we would minister to and I could practically feel the onset of a miracle. My instincts proved to be correct. Nearly 1,300 people showed up on launch weekend. The auditorium overflowed with people and our kids' rooms were filled with smiling and engaged youngsters. I was on a holy high . . . Until I popped my head into the baby room. The volunteers were trying to smile and keep a positive attitude, but nearly every child in the room was screaming. I looked to the leader and she just shrugged. I chalked it up to separation anxiety and a new environment. I reasoned, "Surely, it'll get better with time." It didn't. Eight weeks later, as I made my rounds, I once again popped my head into the baby room. I didn't hear screaming, so I assumed we were seeing improvement. When I looked into the beautiful baby room we had constructed, I saw several volunteers standing around with nothing to do. There were no babies—not a single one. I looked to Kristy, the room leader, and said, "Where did all the babies go?" She again shrugged and said, "I think we scared them off." I was mystified. How had we scared them off? We had a beautiful, clean, safe environment. It was fun and colorful. We had spared no expense with the latest toys and gadgets. We had the sweetest team of volunteers prepared to nurture and care for the smallest of our eKidz. It didn't make sense.

Later that week, I scheduled a time to have coffee with Kristy. I was determined to get to the bottom of this quandary. After nearly twenty minutes of niceties and nudging, she finally confided her suspicions. Kristy said, "Jessica, I think the room, as beautiful as it is, is too bright. Every surface, from the floor to the walls, is covered in neon orange and lime green. I think it may be overstimulating to the babies."

It made sense. We had experienced chaos in that particular room for nearly two months. It was the only room of its kind, and, well, it *was* bright. I immediately commissioned Kristy to tackle the problem. I gave her a budget and said something along the lines of, "I don't care how you do it, just tamper down that color."

I will never forget her wide eyes and stunned expression. "You think I can fix the problem? You trust me enough to spend the money to find a solution." I was equally as stunned. Of course I trusted her. I had installed her as a leader. She was kind, loyal, and hard-working. We ran through a few potential solutions before she left and I put the implementation of our new idea fully in her hands.

I'm happy to report that with the addition of soft lamp lighting and a soothing sound machine, our baby room was back in business the next weekend. One month later, our babies were back. The lesson I learned through that experience was less about bright color palettes and babies and more about empowerment. Leaders and volunteers need constant assurance and guidance. Empowering your team means providing the support and encouragement necessary to execute with excellence and solve problems as they arise. Coaching does just that. It provides on-the-spot feedback that's both constructive and empowering. It enables volunteers to ask questions of a leader they view as their friend and advocate, and to make educated decisions. I often wonder if a Coach would have empowered Kristy to solve the baby room problem long before families stopped showing up.

Whether you choose to install a coaching model or not, I challenge you to put systems in place that allow your volunteers to communicate with you or another high-level leader on a weekly basis. Don't rely on a commitment card to ensure your volunteers' development. Be a source of encouragement. Don't avoid conflict. Create conversations that provide opportunities for growth. Listen to your teams and celebrate the wins. Protect their commitment by creating a safe place for volunteers to take the reins and lead. That's my recipe for empowerment.

12

CHAPTER

THE WHYS AND HOWS OF EMPOWERMENT

Jessica Bealer

"**N**ot again," I mumbled under my breath. "Am I the only one who cares about excellence?" This was the third time I'd relocated the pens from the top of the check-in cart to the drawer organizer in which I felt they belonged. I was just about to go find who was responsible and explain the need for organization when someone cleared her throat behind me.

"Hey, Jessica," Heather said, "can I grab a pen?" I picked one up from the drawer and handed it to her. She smiled and said, "Thanks! They keep disappearing from the top of the cart where I keep them for when I check in first-time guests. I hate having to walk away and look for a pen—it makes me look unprepared." She smiled, took the pen, and walked back to the new family she was assisting.

I don't know if she heard me grumbling or not, but I learned a valuable lesson in that moment. My standards are not God's standards, and if I refuse to empower those I lead to participate in the advancement of God's kingdom, not only am I doing them a disservice, I'm also sacrificing the ministry God has entrusted to me on the altar of my personal preference. My job as a leader is to connect parents, grandparents, kids, students, and volunteers to the power of Jesus and let Him work in their hearts and minds. It's not to hoard power and authority over the able-bodied team God has blessed me with.

Empowering others is tough for most leaders because we have an instinctive need to control everything. When we empower a leader, we've handed over control. Over time I've learned that when I refuse to release the reins, I've reduced the potential of my ministry by the capacity of the person God intended to use. Your ministry's impact is equal to the individuals you empower

YOUR MINISTRY'S IMPACT IS EQUAL TO THE INDIVIDUALS YOU EMPOWER TO SEE IT ACCOMPLISHED. BE SELECTIVE, CHOOSE WISELY, AND THEN TRUST IMMENSELY.

to see it accomplished. Be selective, choose wisely, and then trust immensely.

Need more convincing?

HERE ARE SIX REASONS WHY YOU NEED TO EMPOWER THOSE YOU LEAD.

You Need Fresh Ideas

It took years of experience before I learned the difficult lesson that I don't know everything. I like to have an answer for every question. It's a blessing that often leads to breakdown. Decisiveness is a good skill to have when leading a large organization. However, when I make decisions without consulting others I often find my ideas are dry, ineffective, and lack originality. Inventive initiatives most often come when I hand over creative license to someone who has shown both reliability and eagerness.

You Need More Hands

A few months ago I was slumped over my desk in defeat. It had been weeks since mail that had been returned to our family ministries department had been processed, and the stack felt insurmountable. Honestly, the task was going to take me about two hours, but I was already running behind and two hours was the difference between making my daughter's parent observation night for dance or staring at my computer. I was already coming to terms with the would-be tears, when Rebecca walked by and said hello. Rebecca is an incredible volunteer who homeschools her children and finds time to help around the office. Seeing my situation, she offered to help. I enthusiastically agreed and, in that moment, a magical relationship formed.

Six months later, not only had Rebecca continued to process the returned mail, but she also helped us begin to streamline our processes by tracking the campuses with the most informational errors. It was a good reminder for me. Ministry involves people ministering to other people. If you're the only one marking things off your to-do list, you're hoarding the blessing that comes with doing God's work, and I would speculate those "blessings" feel more like burdens to you. It's time to enlist help. You'll be surprised at the advancements your ministry will make when you choose to empower others.

You Need Recruiters

I've counseled many family ministry leaders over the years, and the most common question I receive is, "How do I get more volunteers?" It's the universal problem when it comes to ministry. Like I said above, you need more hands . . . but where are they and how can you get them plugged in? The best and easiest way to fill those vacant slots is to build strong teams. Let me explain. You love what you do. You probably talk about it nonstop to anyone who will listen. When you grow and nurture your teams to the point of empowerment, you essentially create dozens of passionate megaphones. These individuals will not only advance your ministry but will also recruit family members, coworkers, and even neighbors to come and check out the amazing things they get to be a part of.

You Need to Build Camaraderie

A healthy team is one that laughs and cries together. Their mission is clear and their hearts are aligned. They have inside jokes and take field trips. They send each other birthday cards and give one another Christmas presents. The foundation of a healthy team is trust, but developing trust takes time. It's not something that happens overnight. You can't command your teams to trust one another. However, there is one sure way to communicate you trust those you lead—empower them to make decisions. I can promise you that mistakes will be made and in your frustration you'll beg and plead with yourself to take back control. Don't. When your team members see that you believe in them despite their missteps, a bond will form. Trust says, "I believe in you and I stand with you, no matter what."

You Need to Keep Your Sanity

I once did an exercise in which I identified what was called a "mental model." A mental model is an image or representation of how you see yourself in your current role. If you look at your present position and view yourself as a circus clown that entertains parents and kids and juggles a million tasks and responsibilities to keep the show going, I predict you are only a few days, weeks, or months away from total burnout. Ministry can be overwhelming, and if you're juggling too many balls, maybe it's time to hand a few off. Invite others to join in the fun. Your calling is too important to allow the monotony of weekly tasks to dishearten you or steal your enthusiasm. I do believe there are individuals that are called into a certain role or position for a season, but for most of us, this is a life mission. If you want to still be here 10, 20, or even 30 years from now, you're going to need to learn the art of delegation.

You Need to Replace Yourself

God never intends to leave you where you are. Don't get me wrong, I'm not saying it's time to start looking for another job. What I mean is that you should be consistently growing in wisdom, discernment, knowledge, and capacity. A great leader is never content with the status quo. Your ministry will advance with God's blessing and your initiative. True insight comes when you allow space in your schedule for dreaming. It's hard to dream of what could be when you're constantly bombarded with what is. The only way to make such a shift is to identify leadership potential and urge those individuals to take more responsibility. When you invest and empower those you lead, not only will your teams be stronger, but you'll find time to turn those ministry dreams into reality.

So, if you want to empower those you lead, here are three ways to help you LET GO of the reins:

FIRST, LET GO OF LOOKING AT THE TREES, AND INSTEAD FOCUS ON THE FOREST.

I've said this before because it's a key part of empowerment: Always inspect what you expect. It's not micromanaging to check on an initiative or task that was delegated as long as it's done in love and with the goal to support until completion. However, many of us go to inspect and get trapped in the trivialities of ministry, and no matter what you think, there are trivialities. Just like the pen experience I described at the beginning of this chapter, some things don't matter.

As a leader, it's your job to keep your focus on the big picture. It doesn't mean you don't see the trees, it just means your priority is the forest as a whole. I've spoken to ministry leaders who became so focused on a particular system or aspect of their ministry they didn't see the forest fire of doubt or weariness sweeping through their ministry. When you find yourself hacking away at a broken branch, I would implore you to use what I call the "Rule of Five." Ask yourself, "Will this matter in five hours? In five days? In five years?" Remind yourself this is a marathon, not a sprint. Empowering your teams to handle the small stuff ensures you'll finish the race. Inspect the trees, but never lose sight of the forest.

Action Step: Make a list of five things you need to stop doing right now and hypothesize on who could carry those responsibilities.

THEN, SORT YOUR PRIORITIES AND LET GO OF THE TRIVIAL.

As I mentioned above, there are aspects of your ministry that are less important than others. However, in a busy season when everyone and everything seems to demand your attention, it's often hard to distinguish the crucial from the insignificant. But just because you're the leader doesn't mean you have to be the one who always dishes out the answers. There are certain things only you can speak to. Those need to be your priorities. Here are a couple of personal examples.

I once had a volunteer at a non-permanent location say, "Teardown seems to take a really long time and I just need to get out of here quick so I can spend time with my kids on my day off."

My response: "I understand. I think your leader will as well. Why don't you talk to him and explain your situation. I'm sure you'll be able to find a solution that works for both of you."

Could I have stepped in and made the call to let this volunteer leave early every week? Yes. Did I have the authority to do that? Yes. Would I? No. If I've empowered someone to lead, then I need and expect them to lead. I wouldn't subvert the authority I've delegated with a quick, rash answer to a trivial problem.

At that same non-permanent location, I had a volunteer leader come to me about a different issue. He said, "The janitor is saying he doesn't like cleaning up in the library (a room we used for small group space) and he is cutting our space in half. Do you want to go talk to him, or for me to just make it work in the smaller space?"

My response: "Yes, I'll go speak with him and try to work something out. You need that space. Do you know where I can find him right now?"

Small groups are a priority for the ministry I led, and reducing the space would have put an unnecessary strain on our group leaders and lessened the experience for kids. The janitor was contracted by the church, and as a staff member, I was one of the few people who could talk with him with the appropriate authority. This was a priority.

One of the best ways to grow in this area is to write out everything you do during the week and on the weekend, then highlight the items that are a priority. Everything else needs to be entrusted to capable individuals who understand the vision and can clearly communicate it.

Action Step: Think back over the past month. Name one situation in which you asserted your authority when you could have empowered a leader. Then identify a situation you failed to address because you allowed minor distractions to steal your focus.

AND FINALLY, LET GO OF PERFECTION AND CHOOSE TO REDEFINE FAILURE.

We know the end of the story. Jesus wins! Victory is found in our Savior. However, in the daily grind of ministry, missteps are made, battles are lost, and people walk away. There are days we all question our purpose, moments when we wonder if we're even making a difference. If you're anything like me, you had this vision of what a life in ministry would look like and it doesn't remotely resemble where you find yourself today. Perfection isn't possible, but a scrappy team led by a passionate visionary is definitely attainable. The mistakes will refine you. The losses will deepen your faith.

But don't let that scare you away from empowerment. A healthy team is in sync with one another. They feel secure enough to take risks. I challenge you to redefine failure. It isn't a single blunder or misdirection. Failure is relinquishing your rights to the calling God has placed on your life, losing your fervor to complacency, and overloading your appointment calendar because you fear others will disappoint you. Failure is trying to do it all yourself. Perfection might not be possible, but success is within your reach, and it all starts with empowerment.

Action Step: Make a list of the key volunteers you lead. Under each name, list one or two initiatives you would have them complete in the next six months.

Empowerment sounds like a novel concept. It's much harder in practice. Your ministry feels like an extension of you, like a baby or child that you must tend to, nurture, and protect. It is and it isn't. Your ministry is nothing more and nothing less than people. You should care for them, invest in them, and stand with them when life gets hard. However, it's also the goal of any parent to raise independent adults. One day you may not be there to help make an important decision, and when that moment comes, you need to know your volunteers can assess the situation and land on a solution. Empowerment creates buy-in, and if you're willing to take the risk, it won't be long until you have a family of volunteers that, like you, view the ministry as an extension of themselves.

FAILURE IS RELINQUISHING YOUR
RIGHTS TO THE CALLING GOD HAS
PLACED ON YOUR LIFE, LOSING YOUR
FERVOR TO COMPLACENCY, AND
OVERLOADING YOUR APPOINTMENT
CALENDAR BECAUSE YOU FEAR
OTHERS WILL DISAPPOINT YOU.
FAILURE IS TRYING TO DO IT ALL
YOURSELF. PERFECTION MIGHT
NOT BE POSSIBLE, BUT SUCCESS IS
WITHIN YOUR REACH, AND IT ALL
STARTS WITH EMPOWERMENT.

13

CHAPTER

STRATEGIC
VOLUNTEER
APPRECIATION

Jessica Bealer

I once wrote an article titled "Death to Volunteer Banquets." It was about flipping your mindset from doing big, all-encompassing appreciation events for volunteers to instead focusing on appreciating the investment of each, unique individual. Let's be honest, I probably would have called this chapter something along those lines simply for the shock factor, but I didn't want to scare you away before I convinced you of the absolute necessity of personal and intentional volunteer appreciation.

A healthy team is one that has clear direction, is empowered to do what has been asked of them, and feels honored and appreciated for their contribution. Written as a formula, it looks like this:

Clarity + Empowerment + **Appreciation** = Longevity

Ministry is more efficient and effective with volunteers who understand the "why" and are comfortable with the "how." But to achieve this, we need volunteers to stick around longer than the six to twelve month commitments they agree to when they begin serving in our ministries. We need them to join us in this calling, to help us grow generations of young hearts and minds into fierce warriors of Christ.

Simply knowing what to do and how to do it isn't always enough to inspire years of committed service, and as much as I hate to admit it, a simple "thank you" doesn't go as far as you might expect. In the book *It's Just A Phase*, Reggie Joiner and Kristen Ivy explained the need to care for the team members you lead. They said it this way: "If leaders are expected to show up weekly in the lives of children and teenagers, then you need to show up weekly in the lives of leaders." If you're asking a volunteer to devote precious time during the week to pray for the families they serve, communicate with team members, and adequately prepare a lesson plan, it shouldn't surprise you that your investment into those individuals should be significant.

The predicament that most of us find ourselves in when it comes to honoring our teams is that we often operate from a place of *too little, too late.* For instance, we see a nursery volunteer trying to calm a screaming toddler for the entire length of the worship experience to give his or her parents the opportunity to have an encounter with God in the adult service, and in passing we may offer a smile and a, "Thanks for being patient." But where do you think the volunteer's focus is when he or she, feeling completely exhausted, gets in the car to head home? What do they remember? Does he or she feel empty or fulfilled? In my experience, there are a few strategic actions we can take to make sure it's the latter—a list of do's and don'ts if you will.

DO'S AND DON'TS

DO make it personal.
It's easier to treat your volunteer base as one big body, to equalize them and offer generic and comprehensive thanks for a job well done, a year survived, a banquet of vision and appreciation. The problem with this approach should be obvious to most of us. Each and every volunteer you have is unique. Some like to dress up. Some do not. Some have Thursday nights free. Others have kids and feel overwhelmed with extracurricular activities, and a volunteer appreciation banquet feels like a burden rather than an honor. Personal appreciation means you acknowledge the differences between team members and you cater your efforts to match.

DON'T treat everyone the same.
I once handed out five-dollar Starbucks gift cards to everyone on my preschool team. They were doing a great job and I just wanted to spoil them with a cup of coffee on me. The idea seemed harmless. For some volunteers, this gift was a win! The college student from Room C loved it! She was your typical

young adult living on ramen noodles and working her way
through secondary school. Starbucks was her favorite, and the
gift card was a homerun with her. The middle-aged mother
from Room A? Not so much. She smiled, but I could see her
disappointment when I handed her the card. I later found
out this sweet woman, who led her team well, was a multi-
millionaire with kids in college across the country. Rather than
me paying for her coffee, this incredible volunteer would have
gladly paid for my coffee in exchange for 30 minutes of my time
to get to know her better. However, in an attempt to be efficient,
I had offered her little more than a general nod of recognition.
To truly appreciate your team, you must know each unique
individual. Your team's commitment to families in your ministry
is a reflection of your ability to connect with them on a personal
level.

TRY THIS! When new volunteers sign up to serve, ask them to
fill out a quick survey of their likes—their favorite restaurant
or dessert bar, their top sports team or hobby, or even their
favorite candy bar. That way, you can celebrate that individual
in his or her own unique way when the time comes. Expect
greatness from day one, and be prepared to honor that
dedication.

DO publicly honor sacrifice, initiative, and creativity.
My daughter is a competitive dancer. She travels and competes
all over the Southeast. Her bookshelves are lined with trophies
and medals. Each and every time she's called on stage in
front of her peers to be honored for her accomplishments, she
glows. Her accolades reinforce her commitment. She works
harder, renews her focus, and is compelled to excellence. Your
volunteers are the same. When you acknowledge greatness
publicly, you reinforce the proper standards, clarify your
expectations, and strengthen your stakes.

DON'T applaud mediocrity—challenge it!
In an effort to "hold on" to all your volunteers, have you ever
found yourself praising a volunteer who did little more than
meet your minimum standard? For example, "Thanks for being
here. I know it's hard to get here on time, so I'm just glad you

WHEN YOU
ACKNOWLEDGE
GREATNESS PUBLICLY,
YOU REINFORCE THE
PROPER STANDARDS,
CLARIFY YOUR
EXPECTATIONS, AND
STRENGTHEN YOUR
STAKES.

came." These compliments convey to both the volunteer and the team of volunteers surrounding them that the expectation set for them is nothing more than management and maintenance. If you see greater things in the future for your ministry, then speak to that. Instead of being okay with the bare minimum, offer an alternative viewpoint.

TRY THIS! Schedule a regular "all-vol" rally in which you have an honor segment to systematically and uniquely honor volunteers who are going above and beyond.

DO communicate the connection from volunteer investment to real-life change.

It's often difficult for volunteers to keep the big picture in view while volunteering. When a volunteer is elbow deep in dirty diapers, or trying to remain calm when a fifth grade boy causes a disruption in small group, it can cause doubt to creep in as to the impact he or she is having. That's why it's important to draw direct correlations between each volunteer's role and the life change that is occurring because of them.

DON'T assume they know.

You know what it does to assume. It's probably not appropriate to say here, but you know what I mean. Assuming your team members understand the importance of their roles will, over time, leave you without a team altogether.

Ministry is messy and can often be overwhelming. There are days in which each of us question our calling. Your volunteers are no different. It's often difficult to stay motivated when the chaos that accompanies ministry is surrounding you. If you want your team to be able to endure the lows, you must consistently remind them of the highs. Don't presume they know how their actions are making an impact for the kingdom.

TRY THIS! Touch base with your administrative or data staff and find out the names of the adults who recently made a decision to follow Jesus. Cross-reference those names with the kids and students who attend your ministry. Then in your weekly newsletter or email, brag on the volunteers that serve those families, making it possible for both kids and their parents to have an encounter with Jesus.

DO express gratitude promptly.
When you see someone doing something exceptional, express your gratitude . . . immediately! Be as specific as possible. "I love the way you came up with and implemented that solution!" goes much farther than, "Thanks for doing that." The latter sounds obligatory, where the first feels genuine.

DON'T withhold your praise.
There's no benefit in denying someone appreciation. I'm not suggesting you have to follow volunteers around, saying thank you for every small action. There are minimum expectations in every position, but *every time* you see a volunteer, leader, or peer go above and beyond what has been asked of them, draw attention to it. Make it a big deal! Offer kind words and compliments as often as possible. Not only will it increase the likelihood of a repeated behavior, but showing honor and praise will also elevate your personal disposition and enable you to move forward with a constructive mindset.

TRY THIS! This weekend, take 20 minutes out of your morning routine to do nothing but offer praise. Walk from room to room and find a reason to brag on your teams. An atmosphere of gratitude is an atmosphere of growth.

In First Thessalonians, we find a letter the apostle Paul wrote to the church in Thessalonica. It's an important letter because he covered many topics, ranging from relationships among Christians, the process for mourning those who have died, and even specific issues within the church. However, before he began giving instructions, he started with thanksgiving. In the opening moments of the letter, Paul said, *"We always thank God for all of you and continually mention you in our prayers. We remember before our God and Father your work produced by faith, your labor prompted by love, and your endurance inspired by hope in our Lord Jesus Christ"* (1 Thessalonians 1:2–3 NIV).

As leaders, we should take note of Paul's intentionality. Volunteer instruction and empowerment is a must and clarity is a necessity, but appreciation is your secret weapon. If you want to build teams of volunteers that will serve alongside you for years to come, you must develop a wealth of relational equity. This can only happen when you start from a place of gratitude and thanksgiving.

IF YOU WANT TO
BUILD TEAMS
OF VOLUNTEERS
THAT WILL SERVE
ALONGSIDE YOU FOR
YEARS TO COME,
YOU MUST DEVELOP
A WEALTH OF
RELATIONAL EQUITY.

STRATEGIC VOLUNTEER APPRECIATION

14

CHAPTER

DEVELOPING AN URGENCY FOR GROWTH

Gina McClain

L eadership development is a hot topic in ministry circles today, and rightfully so. To quote Bill Hybels, "When the leader gets better, everyone wins."

But developing as a leader is a long, arduous process. Like training for a marathon requires increasingly more difficult long-distance runs, leadership development necessitates an intentional, repetitive, consistent focus on incorporating the right behaviors that will allow you to maximize your potential.

If leadership development were easy and intuitive there wouldn't be millions of blog posts, TED talks, books, and articles written about it. Few people choose to develop themselves as leaders for one simple reason: it's hard.

And why would we do the difficult thing when we have the easier option of doing nothing?

It's a tough reality to face, but culturally we don't like to do hard things.

I can completely identify. I'm in my mid-40s and starting a new sport: swimming.

Let me be honest. I can't swim.

I mean, I can keep myself afloat. I can avoid drowning. I can fake the freestyle stroke with elegance. You know how that works. You paddle casually to the side of the pool without actually sticking your face in the water, so as to not mess up your makeup. After all, this approach works the same as doing it the "correct" way, right?

Wrong. I try to tell myself it's the same, but the truth remains that I can't swim.

But I need to exercise, and nowadays my knees vehemently protest my running regimen. Like Twisted Sister in tight leather pants, they're not gonna take it anymore.

So, I've got to find a cardio workout that isn't so rough on my joints, and swimming is my best prospect. Yet despite my racer suit, goggles, and lap tracking smart-device, there's no masking my novice status when I slip into the pool.

Learning to swim is awkward. Figuring out how to breathe at the right times without sucking chlorinated water up my nose seems impossible. My first day in the pool, a single lap had me gasping for air!

If only you could be a fly on the wall watching my 11-year-old son give me tips on my stroke, writing out a training plan, and cheering me on when I complete a lap. This isn't a private pool, people. There's a full audience of gym members filtering across the pool deck during these training sessions. It's a humbling experience. There's nothing easy or enjoyable about swimming for me. Everything in me wants to quit.

In fact, it would be a lot easier to just stick with running. It's what I know and a great way for me to keep my fitness level high. Despite the repercussion it inflicts on my knees, I can run for several more years if I just reduce my pace.

But when I take the long view of my health and fitness, I'm compelled to stick with swimming. It increases my stamina and further strengthens my core. And it's actually making me a better runner. So I'm determined to fight through and endure what makes it hard.

I view leadership development the same way. Though it can feel awkward and challenging, learning to incorporate new leadership tools is a game changer for the ministry you lead. But there are four critical postures to embrace when it comes to leadership development. You've got to *own your development, set your pace, get accountability,* and *invite inspiration.*

OWN YOUR DEVELOPMENT
It's truly rewarding to serve in a high-development, high-accountability environment. Though it's relentlessly challenging, I'd choose it any day over a role in which my leader isn't focused on encouraging me to improve.

Yet, I'm aware you could be anywhere on the spectrum of leadership support. Whether your ministry environment ranks high or low on the development scale, the primary driver behind your personal development will always be you.

So if you find yourself in a low-development culture, I want to encourage you. God isn't surprised or worried about it. He simply has an alternate plan for your development. He's leading you to the right resources and people to help you. In fact, what a great season to serve in ministry when you have so many resources at your fingertips through outlets like podcasts, blogs, and books! At the end of the day, your development lies squarely on your shoulders. It is no one else's responsibility.

SET YOUR PACE
Setting your pace has everything to do with planning and taking intentional steps. Planning doesn't have to be elaborate. In fact, it's better if it isn't. Keeping it simple will serve you well. Though it's a gift to have so many resources available to you, it can be overwhelming to know where to start. Consider this:

- **Start with Preference:** Whose voices do you prefer? We all have people we admire for their effectiveness. Who's that leader for you? Identify those leaders and begin to consume the content they produce.
- **Introduce Dissonance:** I have a few people I listen to or read simply because they say things that make me squirm. Sometimes I agree with them. Sometimes I don't. But they attack subjects or ask questions that provoke different perspectives. I like how this makes me better.
- **Crash the Rut:** I am a very predictable person. I often utilize the same tools and avenues to learn and grow.

WHETHER YOUR
MINISTRY
ENVIRONMENT RANKS
HIGH OR LOW ON
THE DEVELOPMENT
SCALE, THE PRIMARY
DRIVER BEHIND YOUR
DEVELOPMENT WILL
ALWAYS BE YOU.

Sometimes I over-utilize them. There have been seasons in which the very avenues that produced great fruit in my life suddenly stop working for me. I've learned that every six to eight months, I have to change up my rhythm. I have to introduce something new, try a different approach, or get out of my comfort zone. It's hard to do, but so beneficial on the other side.

GET ACCOUNTABILITY

As a leader, your greatest asset is the accountability you place in your life. Giving someone permission to ask hard questions. Cracking open the door and giving someone access to dig deeper, hold up a mirror and help you see where you need to stretch and grow.

The unfortunate reality is that as leaders we can go a long time without accountability and still be successful. A lack of intentional accountability does not prohibit someone from learning and growing. But having input is an accelerator.

Like adding an extra shot to your Americano, accountability enhances your leadership journey. As leaders, we need our lenses adjusted. If you're anything like me, you can easily view your circumstances in a way that favors you. It's an easy hole to step in. So find someone you trust that will lean in, ask questions, and help you see things you can't see on your own.

INVITE INSPIRATION

As I mentioned before, today we have access to more leadership content than we can possibly consume, much less apply. Finding a mentor who is a little further down the road than you can be a great benefit to both your ministry and your personal development.

A great mentor or coach can help you determine the most important things to focus on in your world. The everyday demands of ministry have a way of consuming our energy and time, leaving very little margin to focus on what matters most.

Choosing a mentor is a tricky thing, so here are a few things to watch for when choosing one:

An Awareness of Their Home Turf

Do you have the benefit of getting to check out their ministry? To see what they do "boots on the ground"? Anyone can make a personal blog or social media feed look stellar. You might look at them and be really impressed. But walking around in their ministry environments and interacting with their volunteer team will tell you volumes about the quality of their leadership. If you can make it happen, go visit your potential mentor's ministry environments and see their world in action.

Relational Chemistry

You want a mentor/apprentice relationship with someone you can connect with and learn from. You want to ask yourself questions like: *Do I enjoy hanging out with them? When I ask questions, do their responses bring clarity? Do they challenge me to reach higher than I would on my own?*

Resist the temptation to discount this aspect of choosing a mentor. Chemistry is important. If you don't enjoy time with this person, it will be difficult to be vulnerable and open to learning from them.

Signs of Growth

When choosing a mentor who will help you grow as a leader, you want to find someone who displays growth in his or her own life. Do they appear to be as teachable as you strive to be? Though it may benefit you for a while, you won't last long with a mentor that's no longer interested in learning and growing themselves. You're looking for a mentor who has their own game plan for personal development and growth. You're looking for someone that isn't interested in settling for less than the best of who they can become. For as long as someone consumes oxygen on this earth, they aren't finished growing and moving toward whom God created them to be.

As I write, I'm challenged once again to ask myself some hard, uncomfortable questions. Questions about my own pursuit of growth and development. I consider teachability to be one of the strongest attributes I bring to the leadership table. And yet, I can find myself drifting toward complacency when I'm not watching. We have a natural bent toward complacency that we must actively resist in order to develop at the pace and to the degree we wish to grow. It's in our nature.

God has woven within each of us the desire to stretch and reach toward the potential He invested in us. We're genetically wired to grow, aren't we? So don't let the enemy win this battle. Don't let him convince you that where you are is good enough. The enemy of great is good enough and your very DNA begs for the divine greatness God created you to experience.

DEVELOPING AN URGENCY FOR GROWTH IN YOUR VOLUNTEERS

While your personal leadership development is important, there is also a need for urgency around the growth and development of your team.

When you stop to think about it, have you ever talked to a ministry leader who was begging God to make their ministry smaller?

That person may be out there, but they're rare. Most of us are asking God for increase. We want to reach more. Whether that "more" is defined in numbers, depth, or some other quantifier, most ministry leaders are asking God for more.

But the pivotal question to this prayer is, *Can you handle more?* Are you ready for it? Do you have the team, structure, and systems to steward the "more" that God brings?

If the answer is no, then it's time to roll up your sleeves and get to work.

Yes, the labor is hard. Yes, your focus will have to be relentless. But the reward for this type of effort is unmatched.

I would suggest that the majority of ministry leaders reading this book desire to grow their ministry numerically. You simply

GOD HAS WOVEN
WITHIN EACH OF
US THE DESIRE
TO STRETCH AND
REACH TOWARD
THE POTENTIAL HE
INVESTED IN US.

want to reach more people with the gospel message. Whether your prayer for growth centers around numbers rising or spiritual connections deepening (or both!), the opportunity lies squarely in the volunteer structure you put in place.

EVEN THE LONE RANGER HAD TONTO

You are not the Lone Ranger. But even if you were, he didn't do anything alone and neither should you. You were never intended to do ministry by yourself. You need others to help you lead what God has given you to steward.

In fact, I would suggest you apply a numeric ratio to your volunteer leaders much like you follow a ratio for the kids or students you lead. What I mean is, as you lead your ministry, you probably follow some kind of numeric guideline to know that you have enough adults helping you to care for and lead the kids at your church.

That ratio might be 15 students for every 1 adult, 10 kids for every 1 adult, or 7 preschoolers for every 1 adult. No matter how your numbers break down, there's a measuring stick to help you determine if you have the help you need.

We do this because we know that we cannot singlehandedly care for all the kids or students God brings our way. We enlist the help of volunteers to make this happen.

But what about the care and needs of your volunteer team? Have you stopped to consider the structure you have in place to care for them?

In the whirlwind of ministry, this is a function that's easily overlooked. Yet we can agree that most of our volunteers want three simple things: to be needed, to be known, and to be equipped.

In children's ministry, it's not difficult for an adult to feel needed when they see a lone volunteer sitting with a group of 20 kids, desperately trying to maintain engagement, while a group of three boys have their own little game of Twister happening on the side. In that moment, the need for help is obvious.

But once you successfully recruit and train a new volunteer, what system do you have in place to ensure they feel known?

The easy trap is to keep the responsibility of their being "known" squarely on your shoulders. You might feel it's your responsibility to love, encourage, challenge, develop, and shepherd the volunteers on your team.

And if you have no more that 8 to 10 volunteers on your team, that system will work great. But once you exceed this number, you're going to need some help.

It really comes down to simple math. We are only capable of knowing and shepherding a finite number of people. Once we exceed that number, we dilute our ability to lead and shepherd well. So elevating others who are gifted and wired to care for and guide others will amplify your leadership within your ministry.

When you apply this logic, it isn't hard to come up with a practical, strategic way of knowing when you add leaders to your team, where you place them, and what you ask them to do.

Let's break this down.

IDENTIFYING WHEN AND WHERE TO ADD LEADERS TO YOUR TEAM

By applying a 5 to 1 ratio to your leadership structure, you agree that for every 5 volunteers, there will be a volunteer leader responsible for their care and equipping. So if you have 100 volunteers, you should have 20 volunteer leaders (also known as Coaches).

In order to begin seeing this more clearly, try putting your volunteer structure on paper in the form of an organizational chart. Put yourself at the top and then list every person you are directly responsible for leading, equipping, challenging and guiding. If that number exceeds 10-15, you need to pull someone alongside you to help.

Draw that layer into your chart and make it your goal to identify and elevate for that role. Don't be afraid to create another hole to fill this one. The leader you're looking for is likely under your nose. And they are probably looking for ways to help you more.

You can also try doing this exercise this way: Take a paper and pencil and draw out your volunteer team. Draw a triangle in a single column on the right side of the paper to represent each volunteer in your ministry. (If you have multiple service times, we recommend you do this by service time, with one organizational chart to represent each service time you host.)

For every five to ten volunteers, draw a rectangle to the left. For a solid leadership structure, you want an individual filling that rectangle that will live out defined behaviors that ensure the triangles (volunteers) under their care are needed, known, and equipped.

Now, here's how you can take this to the next level. Add 20 percent to the chart.

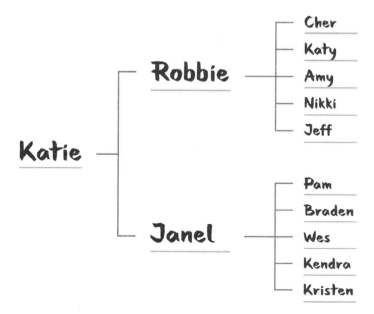

Doing this will move you from being prepared for what God brings you *today* to being prepared for what He wants to bring you *tomorrow*.

If God were to grow your ministry by 20 percent this year, would you be prepared for it?

If God increased your numbers, would you have a plan for how to steward the increase? It's an important question to explore.

If you needed to grow your volunteer team to accommodate 20 percent more than what you currently see, what would your team look like? Draw it out on paper. Create a plan for it today.
- How many additional volunteers do you need?
- How many additional volunteer Coaches will you need?
- Will you need to adjust your check-in process, traffic flow, security measures, and follow-up process?
- How will your communication or training strategy be affected?

There are a variety of ways you can stretch yourself today so you're ready tomorrow. But it requires intentional planning. And intentional planning is what will set you apart as a leader.

Now that you know what your leadership team should look like, you need to consider what it is you'll ask your Coaches to do. How do you lean on them? How can you amplify your leadership through them?

ASKING LEADERS TO DO SOMETHING SIGNIFICANT
Don't fall in the task trap in which the function of your volunteer Coaches is primarily to check items off a list. That's not what a leader is made to do. Don't get me wrong, we should all be willing to do whatever is necessary in the moment.

But, just like you, your leaders will not be satisfied for long if their primary function is to operate from a list of tasks. They want something significant to lead. And it's your job to empower them to do something meaningful.

It can be challenging to figure out what you can ask a volunteer to do. I mean, ultimately, isn't all this stuff *your* job?

The short answer is no. It's not your job to do everything. It's your job to empower others to use their gifts and experiences to carry out the mission. The quality of your ministry will be so much better when you share this responsibility with others. But what exactly should you ask a volunteer leader to do?

There was a moment in my ministry when I realized different people had different definitions of the word "leader." The qualities I might look for in a potential leader were different from the qualities someone else might look for. As a result, there was little to no consistency in the type of leader I recruited for my ministry. We needed to get everyone on the same page and speaking the same language so we could move in the same direction.

Getting there wasn't as difficult as you'd think. It boiled down to a very simple question.

Pulling together some of the key influencers in my ministry, we asked the question, **"Who are our best volunteers—the ones we wish we could put on the copy machine and replicate?"** We all have "that" volunteer, right? But have you ever stopped to ask what makes "that" volunteer so great?

When we took some time to identify our best volunteers, there were a handful of names on our dry erase board. When we applied the question, "What makes them so great?" there were a few qualities—or what we call behaviors—that seemed to be consistent from one volunteer to the next.

When we agreed on the common behaviors that are replicable, we made these our measuring stick. Fighting to keep things simple, we only allowed for five behaviors to hit that list. Though we could have added more, we agreed these five were essential to the function of a great volunteer leader.

These behaviors are:

- **Engages with Team**: Leader engages with their team beyond the weekly worship services
- **Communicates Proactively**: Leader strives to keep leadership informed of what's happening within their team
- **Leads Area and Empowers Others**: Leader actively equips their team with tools for success in their roles
- **Can-Do Attitude**: Leader stands on the solution side of a problem
- **Recruits Others**: Leader actively invites others to be part of the work God is doing in their ministry area

As we look for high-capacity volunteer leaders, we watch for these behaviors. When we discover someone that seems to live out these behaviors, we invite them to consider a volunteer leader role. In recruiting conversations, we ask for their commitment to these qualities and we actively bring accountability to these behaviors throughout the year.

Accountability is a key component to this process. Without accountability, it simply won't work. But that's true of a lot of systems in which someone is stretched beyond their comfort zone. If you fail to bring accountability to a process that encourages growth, you short-circuit it. Accountability is the one thing that keeps people from fading so far from the objective that there's little point in recovering.

In this scenario, accountability comes in the form of a quarterly assessment. Each quarter we take a look at every volunteer leader (a.k.a. Coach) and ask ourselves how he or she is doing with each behavior. We measure based on a scale of one to five—one meaning the individual is under-performing and five indicating the individual is consistent in the five leadership behaviors.

Sometimes we invite the volunteer leader to self-evaluate by asking them how they feel they're performing in each behavior. The exercise alone reminds the volunteers that these behaviors matter to us. There are many things a volunteer leader can do that are great, but if they don't do these five things, they're not winning!

This level of accountability has empowered and challenged our leaders to effectively care for the volunteers on their teams. The accountability has brought about creative solutions and new ways to equip leaders. Shortly after pressing into these behaviors, we received increased requests for contact information and report data so leaders could provide adequate follow-up to those on their teams.

Don't be afraid to ask a leader to do something big. If God wove the gift of leadership within them, they are looking for an outlet to use it. They want to do something significant. Lean in and give them the opportunity.

Don't shy away from accountability. Again, if you have the right people in place and you have solid relationships with them, they'll come to expect it. You've already asked them to take on these tasks. They've agreed to do them. Holding them accountable to how they are doing is the natural next step.

HELPING OTHERS IDENTIFY THEIR NEXT STEP

This is a lesson that's been hard for me to learn. I think it's because things around me move so quickly—once I get a leader in place I no longer want to worry about what happens in that role. I want that Coach to lead and I want to keep moving forward.

But if I'm not careful, I can easily miss what God is doing in the heart of that leader. Even with regular interactions and communication, if I don't ask the right questions I risk missing where God might be leading. That's why it's crucial for me to circle back to the leaders under my care and ask some pointed questions.

First, I ask the leader, *"What is God showing you about what He wants you to do?"*

I've added this to my list of questions I want to explore with each of my leaders. It took me a long time to realize its value. It isn't just a passive question. It's an assumptive question that God is at work in the heart of your leader. He is continually

DON'T BE AFRAID TO
ASK A LEADER TO
DO SOMETHING BIG.
IF GOD WOVE THE
GIFT OF LEADERSHIP
WITHIN THEM, THEY
ARE LOOKING FOR AN
OUTLET TO USE IT.

leveraging the gifts He wove in that leader to impact other people. To think anything less is to miss the work God is doing in them.

When I ask this question, I learn more about the individual on a personal level, but I also learn how I might be able to help . . . even if it means moving them away from my ministry. For some readers, the idea of helping a solid leader move off of your team makes you cringe a little. But let me challenge that response.

First, by helping a volunteer on my team pursue where God is moving their heart, I am partnering with God in His work. By refusing to help (or ignoring the problem), I miss the opportunity to take part in that work. I don't know about you, but I choose to partner.

Here's some good news: When God moves on a leader's heart, it doesn't always mean He's leading them out of where they are. Maybe He's leading them to dig deeper and invest more right where they're at. But they may not see that opportunity clearly. Asking this question gives you insight into what God is doing in the heart of your leaders.

Then I ask them something that prepares me to capitalize on what God is already doing, *"What is God showing you about the ministry you lead?"* Your ministry is evolving and changing. And this is a good thing. The last thing you want is to have leaders who are willing to let programming or methods stagnate.

But the constant nature of change forces us to pay attention to how things are shifting. By observing how things are changing in your ministry, you can begin to predict and prepare for growth opportunities. In addition, you'll want to invite high-capacity leaders into the conversation about how you can continue to grow and improve.

It's important to note this isn't the task of addition by adding more entry-level volunteer opportunities. This is the task of multiplication by looking for more leadership opportunities.

Awareness of growth opportunities means you will be prepared to respond when God is moving in the heart of your volunteer. Knowing *when* a leader is ready for more is great. Knowing *where* you can give them more is strategic.

After asking these first two questions of the Coach I'm meeting with, I then ask myself, *"What is God showing me about this leader?"*

What do you see in them?

Sometimes a leader will ask for more. Maybe it's because they are ready for more. Maybe it's because they are restless. It's important that you discern between the two.

I often confuse restlessness with readiness.

This is probably because I love when someone says they are hungry for more. It excites me when a volunteer decides they want more responsibility. Maybe because I identify with that desire.

But the desire for more doesn't indicate readiness for more.

I lead best when I resist the urge to react impulsively and add greater responsibility to a leader. I lead best when I stop, take time, and actually examine whether or not this person is ready for increased responsibility. The best indicator of future success is current success.

How are they doing in their current role? Are the volunteers they lead flourishing or languishing? What do the volunteers on their team say about the level of support and encouragement they receive? The evidence of a strong leader is in the team they lead.

Don't be afraid to take a magnifying glass and look closely at their work. It will tell you whether or not they are ready for more.

THE EVIDENCE OF A STRONG LEADER IS IN THE TEAM THEY LEAD.

So, ask the questions. Put it on your quarterly task list. Paint it on your office wall. Adopt the posture of consistently asking, "What is God showing my leaders?" and, "What is God showing me?" This posture will foster a culture of development within your team.

15

CHAPTER

BECOMING THE LEADER MY TEAM NEEDS ME TO BE

Jessica Bealer

Fresh out of college, with the ink still wet on my diploma, I accepted a position as marketing director for a local credit union. It wasn't my specialty, but I had taken several marketing classes and was convinced I could employ the strategy of "fake it 'til you make it."

I interviewed with a team of high-level leaders in the organization, one of which was the sitting president, Mr. Underwood. He didn't say much. He would smile, nod his head, and occasionally compliment me on my answer to a particular question. The interview seemed to go well but, again, I didn't have any experience in marketing. I was sure the position would go to someone more qualified.

When I got the call back, I was floored. Not only had I landed the job, but they wanted me to start the next day. And if that wasn't intimidating enough, the president wanted to personally meet with me on my first day.

When I arrived that morning and sat outside Mr. Underwood's office, I was a bundle of nerves. When his secretary finally invited me back I was nearly to the point of confessing my inexperience and lack of know-how. However, as I took a seat in a classic, green, leather high-back, I will never forget what Mr. Underwood said to me.

"I'm confident you're going to do a great job for this organization. You want to know why?"

Stunned, I nodded.

I had full intentions of giving it my all, but his confidence in me was both heartening and perplexing. He barely knew me. How could he have so much confidence in my skills when I had so little?

"You were bright and cheery in your interview, well-spoken, and obviously intelligent, but that's not why I hired you. I hired you because you spoke about your son and your husband nine times during your interview. You are committed to your family and while I value that kind of loyalty, I also realize that you don't work for me." Now I was really confused. Of course I worked for him. My face must have revealed my confusion.

"You work for your family. Your quality of work determines your advancement, and your advancement determines the quality of life you can build for your family. You work for your family, and because I know you're loyal to them, I have no doubt you will show that same loyalty to this organization."

I was blown away.

He had nailed my motivations on the head. He understood my priorities and spoke to them. He also set high expectations that I knew he would hold me accountable for. He was the first leader, outside of my own father, that I remember thinking, "I want to spend as much time learning from him as possible."

If I were to ask you, "Who inspired you to do what you do, to find your purpose in ministry?" you would undoubtedly name a great leader. Someone who challenged and encouraged you, who identified potential within yourself that you couldn't see, someone who offered perspective and accountability.

Great leaders come with different personalities, mannerisms, and approaches. Some are loud and bold in their authority. Others are soft spoken and prevail through servant leadership. Most fall somewhere in the middle, having little to say except when words of wisdom offer a point of view that brings unity and direction. Every leader is different, but all the great ones seem to have a secret sauce that sets them apart. Great leaders draw others to themselves unintentionally. They know just what to say and when to say it, and most of them make it look easy.

When I think back to that first encounter I had with my new boss, I remember being blown away by how in touch he was with his employees. I remember feeling that advancement through hard work and dedication was not only possible, but expected. I also remember feeling a great devotion, not only to my organization, but also to the man who had hired me. He recognized me as an individual, spoke to my potential, and I wanted nothing more than to exceed those expectations.

Over the years, I've developed a strategy for leadership. You might call it a leadership "job description." If you're reading this book, you are most certainly a leader to someone, somewhere, in some capacity. The goal of every leader is to consistently raise up other leaders. If you are struggling to build a healthy team because those you rely on often become disheartened, weary, or bitter, there may actually be a gap in your leadership "job description."

To effectively grow your ministry, you must first clarify the vision, inspire action, create momentum, and expand capacity. But it's not enough to stop there. Once capacity has been expanded and new initiatives are in place, it's time to start again. Clarify the vision. Inspire action. Create momentum. And finally, expand capacity. It's an ongoing cycle that will grow your ministry and advance God's kingdom.

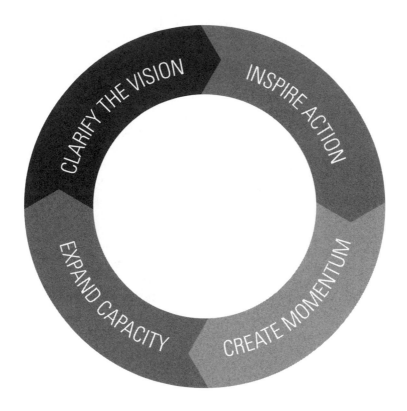

However, this ministry strategy is only effective if your leadership "job description" is designed to raise up those you lead. Throughout the cycle, you should constantly be raising up leaders and replacing yourself.

The solution to every setback I experience starts with me. When I find my ministry failing, or even just taking a few steps in the wrong direction, I begin to self-evaluate. Kingdom-building leaders show consistent similarities in their leadership. Using the acronym RAISE, here are five ways to evaluate your effectiveness as a leader.

ARE YOU RESPONSIVE?

A great leader dispels uncertainty. He or she responds to questions, concerns, or ideas promptly. It's not enough to ask for feedback. Those you lead should feel acknowledged and considered when decisions need to be made.

Ask yourself . . .

- Do I return calls and answer emails in a timely manner?
- Do I hoard information or do I share details as soon as they are available to me?
- Do I discount others' ideas or do I listen and consider implementation?
- Do I have a system for those I lead to offer feedback on a weekly basis?

ARE YOU APPROACHABLE?

Passion activates creativity. Most leaders want passionate people on their teams, but is your demeanor actually diverting creative solutions? When you're accessible, open-minded, and amicable, team members will eagerly bring suggestions and proposals to you.

Ask yourself . . .

- Am I social and friendly?
- Am I confrontational or easy to talk to?
- Do I ask questions and offer compliments freely?

ARE YOU INVESTED?

When you choose to invest in someone you lead, you intentionally carve out time and put forth effort to see them successfully reach the next level of leadership. If it's not personal to you, it's not a true investment. Dividends require risk and a sacrifice on the part of the investor.

Ask yourself . . .
- How much time do I spend each week with those I lead?
- Do I consistently speak vision?
- Do I offer constructive feedback?

ARE YOU SUPPORTIVE?

You've heard the saying *when life gives you lemons, make lemonade*. It's easier said than done. Like lemons, life can sometimes be sour and messy. Those you lead need to know you will be with them through whatever comes their way. Supporting your team means knowing them, loving them, and doing life alongside them.

Ask yourself . . .
- Do I seek to know the individuals who make up my team?
- Am I committed to seeing my team through the highs and lows of life and ministry?
- Do I celebrate the successes of those I lead?

ARE YOU EMPOWERING?

In the beginning there was one leader: you. And that's a fine place to start. However, unless you identify capable people, delegate the work, and encourage ownership, your ministry will also finish with one.

The life span of your ministry is directly linked to your ability to pick up and release tasks and initiatives. Those you lead need to know you trust them. They need to feel comfortable making important decisions. At some point, you were given the opportunity to lead and you made the most of it. Those on your team are ready and waiting for the same opportunity.
Don't allow your fear of failure to rob others of their calling.

Ask yourself . . .
- Do I authorize team members to brainstorm and implement solutions?
- Do I micromanage or encourage ownership?
- Do I vocalize my trust often?

As your ministry grows, you'll want to divide yourself into eighths and keep juggling everything. For most of us, there's an innate need for control. However, by doing this your ministry will be limited by your own flaws, weaknesses, and capacity. Great leaders raise up other leaders, and the greatest leaders are neither envious nor bitter when their apprentices surpass them.

As you pour into the Coaches and leaders around you, remember to be:

R esponsible
A pproachable
I nvested
S upportive
E mpowering

The product of healthy leadership is the development of great leaders. If you look at those who have been placed in your charge and they are no further along in their spiritual or mental maturity and have experienced zero increase in capacity, it might be time to make a change in your leadership style. Imagine the generational impact you could have if every year you were shaping and producing leaders who are approachable, invested, supportive, and empowering.

Your responsibility to those you lead goes beyond problem-solving and inspirational rhetoric. When you step into a leadership position, an unspoken agreement exists between you and those you lead. With their commitment and your investment, they too will grow and develop into the kind of leaders that get mentioned in thank you speeches and book manuscripts.

GREAT LEADERS RAISE UP OTHER LEADERS, AND THE GREATEST LEADERS ARE NEITHER ENVIOUS NOR BITTER WHEN THEIR APPRENTICES SURPASS THEM.

16

CHAPTER

GET GRIT

Gina McClain

T he story of Nehemiah resonates with me. If you've never read the story, I highly recommend that you do. It's a fascinating story of one man's efforts to create change among a group of resigned, defeated, and hopeless Israelites.

I admire many aspects of Nehemiah's character, but I can't say I always emulate them in my own life. Like how his strategic interaction with the king ensured that when the opportunity presented itself, Nehemiah was ready with a list of requirements that needed to be met in order to accomplish his goal.

I will probably spend the rest of my leadership career striving to improve my ability to plan ahead and prepare. Unfortunately, my procrastinator gene often gets the best of me.

But there's a moment in Nehemiah's story when he was faced with a threat that would end not only his ministry, but his life as well. As he led the Israelites to rebuild the defenses around their city, every stone placed in the wall brought greater security against the threat of harm. But every stone placed in the wall also angered their neighboring enemies.

Efforts to stop the work only resulted in frustration. Until finally Israel's neighboring leaders tried to put a stop to the rebuilding once and for all. They sent one of their best leaders, Sanballat, to apply pressure and scare Nehemiah away from his mission.

Nehemiah knew their motives. He knew the intentions behind their veiled invitation to "talk." When I read the story of Nehemiah, what I admire most is his unrelenting focus.

I think most people would have stopped working on the wall.

But Nehemiah was smart enough not to go with Sanballat and his cronies. At the threat of physical harm, most people would opt to pull back, lay low, and wait out the danger. Not Nehemiah.

He was so sold out to the mission—so driven with vision—that the threat of physical harm only amplified the need to drive it to completion. He even said, "Why should the work stop while I leave it and go down to you?" (Nehemiah 6:3 NIV).

In other words, he was saying, "Why should I allow myself to be distracted by you? What I'm doing is valuable. And you are nothing more than a distraction."

I can't begin to count the number of "on the wall" moments I've had in ministry. To be transparent, my greatest struggle in ministry is feeling inadequate. With a track record packed full of mistakes, it's an emotional wrestle to believe that I can complete the task God has placed before me.

Left unchecked, my inner dialogue is wrought with doubt and fear. There have even been moments when that mentality threatened to take me out of the game.

Like this one time many years ago, when I was a few years into my role leading the kids ministry at a multi-site campus. It was the end of a long day and I was packing my things, preparing to head to my final meeting of the day. The last minute meeting request had come earlier that morning, but it wasn't a surprise. The person who sent the invite wanted to know if I could meet at 4:00 p.m. at the central offices.

Seeing the recipients of the meeting request, the purpose of the meeting was no mystery. For months, tension had mounted between myself and another staff member on the team. The changes she insisted needed to happen at my campus were not as simple to resolve as she proposed. And my own inability to deal with conflict resulted in a growing frustration between the two of us.

Our leader had finally had enough and was ready to find a resolution.

My defenses were up from the moment I entered the room. From my perspective, my coworker sitting across the room seemed to have all the control. I felt like I had none.

As we volleyed our points back and forth, the debate grew increasingly intense. Finally I decided I was done. To continue the debate meant I might not win. To concede my point and yield meant I might have to try something I wasn't sure I could accomplish. I faced uncertain failure.

In a moment of exasperation, I stared down the table at my leader, and stated, "I'd rather flip hamburgers than work for you any longer."

I then stood up and left the building.

One mile down the road I ran out of gas. The only person I could think to call was one of my closest friends who'd been sitting next to me in that meeting.

The drive home was icy and silent. I didn't want to talk about it. I knew I was in the wrong. But my fear of failure had erupted like Mount Vesuvius. Quitting on the spot might be failure, but at least it was a failure I chose. Trying to lead through something I wasn't sure I could accomplish . . . that was control I didn't think I could relinquish.

It didn't take long before my campus pastor called me. Though I wanted to dig my heels in, I knew I didn't want that to be the end of the story.

With humility, I spent the next week personally apologizing to everyone impacted by my outburst. I made a commitment to work things out with the person at the center of the struggle. I agreed to meet with her each week to talk through the concerns she had. Each conversation opened the door to greater understanding on both sides.

Ironically, that intentional time revealed we had a shared passion to equip and encourage parents. As time progressed, we leveraged each other's influence to implement change in our ministry areas.

I think this is why I white-knuckle this moment in Nehemiah's life. It's a buoy for me in the midst of some of my wildest leadership storms. He embodied sheer tenacity and courage by continuing his work despite the risk. I want the same tenacity to define my leadership. He had the willingness to bear down and push through regardless of the storm around him and with no fear of the unknown outcome.

I think the reason so many ministry leaders throw in the towel has as much to do with control as fear. Like a symbiotic relationship, control can't survive without fear and fear can't survive without control.

Year after year I watch ministry leaders with great potential surrender and slink back into the shadows because of fear. *What if I can't succeed? What if this is too hard? What if I make a fool of myself?*

The truth is, if I ever leave the battle, I want to go on my own terms. Not someone else's.

I don't think I'm alone in that.

Fear could drive me to step back and guarantee failure, but at least it would be my call. I would control how and when. It's not right thinking, but it's how I can see things when my focus is off.

But courage requires that I take the risk no matter the outcome. Courage drives me to step into the ring. Courage drives me to stay on the wall and continue working with no guarantee of the outcome.

It's risky. It's dangerous. It's scary.

I THINK THE REASON
SO MANY MINISTRY
LEADERS THROW IN
THE TOWEL HAS AS
MUCH TO DO WITH
CONTROL AS FEAR.
LIKE A SYMBIOTIC
RELATIONSHIP,
CONTROL CAN'T
SURVIVE WITHOUT
FEAR AND FEAR
CAN'T SURVIVE
WITHOUT CONTROL.

WE DON'T LEAD IN A BUBBLE. WHEN WE CHOOSE TO REMAIN ON THE WALL— TO FACE WHAT NEEDS TO BE FACED, OPEN OURSELVES UP, AND BECOME RIDICULOUSLY TEACHABLE— THOSE WE LEAD ARE INSPIRED TO DO THE SAME. GRIT IS CONTAGIOUS.

But it's worth it.

Because remaining and fighting through the fear develops a relentless tenacity and focus that's inspiring. Not just personally inspiring, but corporately moving as well.

I mean, think about it. There was a point at which half of the Israelites stood watch while the other half worked on the wall. It wasn't a secret that their lives were at risk.

I would suggest that Nehemiah's unwillingness to be distracted, his insistence to continue working despite the danger, and his stubborn belief that God is greater than anything that might have threatened their success was a corporate inspiration to those who worked beside him.

We don't lead in a bubble. When we decide to stick our heads in the sand and pretend we don't need to grow, everyone around us suffers. But when we choose to remain on the wall—to face what needs to be faced, open ourselves up, and become ridiculously teachable—those we lead are inspired to do the same. *Grit* is contagious.

So we've established the necessity and benefits of developing grit in our leadership. But the next question is, *how do we do we do it?* How do we develop this stick-to-it, not-going-to-quit attitude when we encounter challenges?

STEP 1: RECOGNIZE THE STORY YOU'RE TELLING.
Research revealed in the book *Crucial Conversations: Tools for Talking When Stakes Are High* says we all tell ourselves a story. I've got one running in my mind all the time. The story I tell myself informs my actions on a daily basis. The problem comes when the narrative in my head is inaccurate. And many times, that's the case.

This isn't intentional. We just have gaps in our stories that we fill with opinion and conjecture. If we never correct those gaps with fact, then we end up making decisions with incomplete perspectives.

This reality means we should take care not to react too quickly to circumstances that seem insurmountable. If we don't learn to capture those stories in our heads and correct them, we run the risk of "snowballing the story" and convincing ourselves the role we are in is no longer the role for us. Eventually we decide the grass is greener somewhere else and we move on.

A good practice I've discovered to prevent a poorly planned reaction in these situations is to apply a defined "time to impact" equation to the circumstance.

I borrowed this from a spending strategy I learned from my senior pastor many years ago. Here's how it works. When it came to money management, my senior pastor advocated for a "time to dollars" approach. For any purchase over 100 dollars, the more dollars an item cost, the greater amount of time you took to think and pray. For example, a purchase of 500 dollars would require 5 days of consideration. An expense of 1,000 dollars would necessitate 10 days. The purpose of the equation is to create space and time to think clearly and seek wisdom, avoiding an emotionally-driven decision you'll later regret.

We can apply the same strategy to the circumstances we face. The greater the impact, the more time and space you should give yourself to think, pray, and seek wise guidance.

These steps can ensure you will fill in the gaps in your story with facts, equipping you to make the right decision and not act rashly.

STEP 2: IDENTIFY WHAT STORY YOU WANT TO TELL.
In all transparency, this step has prevented me from quitting on countless Mondays over the past 16 years. Of all the strategies I've employed to develop grit, I've leaned on this tool the most.

When I stop for a moment and put myself on the other side of a problem, I can hear Andy Stanley in my head asking me, "What story do you want to tell?"

Every time I've asked myself this question, my desire to tell a story of perseverance and faith is overwhelming. Answering this question forces me to be specific about the outcome I want to see. The way I want to grow. Answering this question helps me lower my defenses and embrace a teachable posture. When I'm really struggling, I've found that writing out my answer to that question increases my motivation to adapt and grow.

STEP 3: INVITE OBJECTIVE PERSPECTIVES.

When you're in the middle of a hard situation, you can't see things clearly. And the most dangerous thing you can do is to establish your position by leaning on a subjective fan base.

We all have a fan base—those people in our lives that would defend us to the core. You know, people like your mom, your spouse, or your dog. It isn't that they are incapable of being objective, they just don't come by it easily when it comes to you. And that's okay. We all need a fan base cheering us on no matter the odds.

But it's critically important to have some people in your life that are capable of objectivity. Sure, they're still cheering you on toward success. But they're able to step back and help you see the big picture more clearly.

I have that person in my life.

"How many times are you going to circle this mountain, Gina?"

The statement hit me between the eyes. I was on the phone confiding in a long-distance friend trying to explain my position on a situation I was facing. The problem was she'd already heard this story before. The dates had changed, the people involved were different, but the problem was one I'd faced in the past.

"Gina, you can continue justifying your position and convincing yourself you're right. And in some respects, you are right. But that doesn't mean you have nothing to learn here. It looks to me like God has brought you back around the mountain again. He's giving you the opportunity to face this and work through it, if you're ready. And if you're not, He'll just take you around the mountain again. Why not just work through it now and save yourself the trip!"

This was hard to hear. And yet I needed to hear it. My dog isn't objective enough to give me such wisdom, so I need people in my life that are.

My litmus test for determining whether or not I need to seek objective guidance is to look for the times when I don't want to. The minute I find myself in a situation and I'm tempted to move away from objective perspectives, that's when I know I need it most. That's when I know I'm dangerously close to insulating myself and missing an opportunity to grow.

STEP 4: UNDERSTAND THE CYCLE.
There's no denying it. There's a cycle every leader walks through. It's a process of development—a general timeline that's consistent from one person to the next. You can almost predict when a leader is going to grow discontent, disenchanted, or disillusioned with their role. Let me explain.

Consider what the typical ministry leader walks through in the first four years of ministry.

Year 1
Your jokes are funny. Your ideas are fresh. Your perspective is new. It isn't that you're flawless. There's just a lot of grace for those flaws as everyone around you is trying to adjust their own ways of interacting to match yours.

Year 2
Your consistency in the ministry has earned you more equity and people are beginning to trust you more. You still have a lot of ideas you want to implement, but you're getting better at recognizing the most important ideas to chase first.

But you've also hit a few walls recently that you just can't break through or even find your way around. There was a conflict with a volunteer that you just can't get on board, and a disconnect with the student pastor that prevented you from truly working together. Oh, and a disagreement with your senior pastor you're unwilling to address. But these brick walls aren't a big deal; they're nothing you can't set-aside for now. It's not as if they prevent you from doing ministry . . . Right?

Year 2.7

Your jokes are growing redundant and you realize you need a new source for material. Your ideas all seem to sound the same and you need to find a way to break out of the rut. But you're beginning to see some fruit from some of the earliest changes you made. This is exciting except for the fact that the walls you ran into earlier in your tenure are growing too large to ignore. In fact, no amount of effort seems to make them go away. You've tried a few things to change and grow through them but nothing seems to work. Everywhere you turn, you encounter these problems and you can't get away from them. You begin to believe you're not cut out for the job or not a good fit for your team. You might begin to believe they need a leader with a different personality, more experienced skill set, or easier-going mojo.

Year 3.5

You start entertaining the idea of moving somewhere else. You actually respond to one of those scouting emails you keep getting that talk about ministry opportunities in a neighboring community . . . or across the continent. I mean, you're just not successful here. Yes, you've been able to accomplish a few things. The ministry you lead is stronger than when you came. But your senior leader keeps holding you accountable for things you view as impossible to accomplish. You've got a few volunteers that seem to have it out for you and you just can't get them on your side. And your job would be so much easier if you didn't have to share space with the student pastor with locust-like teenagers that converge on the building once a week, devour everything, and move on.

Year 3.9

You've discreetly explored a few opportunities outside your church and now you've made your decision. You believe God has led you out to a new season of ministry and it's time to share the news. You drop the bomb on your senior pastor on Monday morning. By the end of the week you've shared your transition with your volunteer team and it's time to make the news public. The next few months your social media profiles are filled with tweets of anticipation as you move to what God has next. #GodisGood

Year 4
Your jokes are funny. Your ideas are fresh. Your perspective is new. It isn't that you're flawless. There's just a lot of grace for those flaws as everyone around you is trying to adjust their own ways of interacting to match yours . . . Sound familiar?

Don't get me wrong. I realize this doesn't apply to every transition we see in ministry. I'm not suggesting that. But I am suggesting that every ministry leader encounters personal leadership challenges that they struggle to grow beyond. And if they lack the opportunity, space, and accountability to grow beyond them, they won't stick it out.

They will simply find another place and hit the reset button.

The problem with the situation is that there are aspects to leadership growth that are cyclical. Like the classic *Competency Cycle*, there are stages we walk through as we develop as leaders.

The point at which most leaders fade into the sunset is that phase between consciously incompetent and consciously competent.

Once you decide you want to grow beyond the problem, you have to find the resources and accountability to help you. Then you have to do the hard work of stretching yourself. This can be a long and arduous process. And most people just don't want to do it.

Most people would rather make a change and attempt to start over again.

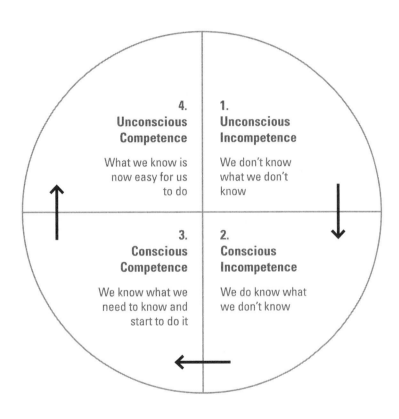

DEVELOPING GRIT IN OUR
LEADERSHIP BEGINS WITH
UNDERSTANDING THERE IS A CYCLE
WE WILL GO THROUGH AS WE GROW
AND LEARN. NO ONE STEPS INTO
MINISTRY AND KNOWS EVERYTHING
THEY NEED TO KNOW. WE'VE ALL
HAD TO DO THE HARD WORK OF
DISCOVERING OUR INCOMPETENCE,
OWNING IT, AND WORKING TO
DEVELOP THE SKILLS TO MOVE
TOWARD COMPETENCE. IN FACT, IF
WE'RE HONEST, WE'RE STILL DOING
THAT HARD WORK TODAY.

But moving doesn't guarantee you get away from these problems. In fact, you're bound to encounter these problems again. It's only a matter of time.

But that doesn't have to be your story. You don't have to start over just so you can end up in a new place with different faces, but the same problems.

You don't have to circle the mountain over and over again. You can tackle this challenge now.

Developing grit in our leadership begins with understanding there is a cycle we will go through as we grow and learn. No one steps into ministry and knows everything they need to know. We've all had to do the hard work of discovering our incompetence, owning it, and working to develop the skills to move toward competence. In fact, if we're honest, we're still doing that hard work today.

As long as you draw breath, you will always discover areas where you can grow. So, set your mind to the task, stay on that wall, and build it brick by brick by brick.

17

CHAPTER

KNOWING YOUR
WHY

Jessica Bealer

H ow many times have you quit on Monday? Maybe you didn't march into your pastor's office with a letter of resignation, but you woke up thinking, "I can't do this anymore." My husband and I have a long-standing joke about the need for a book titled *It's Monday, I Quit.* Mondays are tough for everyone, but especially for those of us in ministry. There are a dozen problems from the weekend that need to be handled, awkward phone calls to apologize for an overlooked policy, and the remains of tense moments between colleagues whose priorities don't always align. Oh, and don't forget, you get to do it all over again in six days.

That's why we named this book, *DON'T QUIT!* If you picked up this book and started reading because you were looking for a lifeline, I want to take a moment to state the obvious: Jesus is your lifeline. God is your portion. You don't do what you do to please other people. You wake up each morning with a single purpose, to use the skills and abilities that God has graciously given you to advance the kingdom of God and make the name of Jesus famous. With that being said, endurance requires clarity. If you plan to be used by God to advance His kingdom, it's necessary to have a clear understanding of not only *what* you do, but also *why* you do it.

WHAT'S YOUR WHY?

Despite the Monday morning blues, there have probably been times when you've said, "I have the best job in the world!" And in those moments you whole-heartedly meant it. You love what you do, or at least you're in love with the idea of what you do. Investing in the next generation ensures the continuation of the gospel. That should be motivation enough, right? Unfortunately,

ENDURANCE
REQUIRES CLARITY.
IF YOU PLAN TO
BE USED BY GOD
TO ADVANCE HIS
KINGDOM, IT'S
NECESSARY TO
HAVE A CLEAR
UNDERSTANDING OF
NOT ONLY WHAT YOU
DO, BUT ALSO *WHY*
YOU DO IT.

as we talked about above, it's not. I'm not saying you shouldn't have an emotional connection to your ministry. But I am saying your calling is more than a vague and overarching purpose statement. Your *why* has to be specific to you. What keeps you up at night? What gets your heart racing? What singular topic occupies your thoughts and the majority of your conversations?

For me, it's that I want kids to grow up loving church. More specifically, I want church to be a safe place that brings a smile. I want it to be a breeding ground for healthy relationships. I want my kids and others just like them to know that Jesus loves them and the church is for them no matter what. That's my *why*.

A well-known philosopher once said, "He who has a why can endure any how." It's easy for leaders to get caught up in the "what" or "how" of ministry. We have software that keeps us on task. We create to-do lists and milestones that help us meet deadlines. These are great tools as long as our target hasn't shifted. When asked, you shouldn't have to think about why you do what you do. Your *why* is the foundation on which you build your ministry. Your *why* is your calling.

In Latin, the word *inspire* means "to breathe life into." If your purpose isn't as apparent as it should be, I encourage you to go back to the beginning and ask yourself, "Why did I choose this? What inspired me to take action? What did I intend to breathe life into?"

HERE ARE FIVE REASONS WHY IT'S IMPORTANT TO KNOW YOUR WHY.

1. Motivation
In his book *Start With Why,* Simon Sinek states, "Your why is your purpose, cause, and belief—it's what's driving your motivation for action." When you don't know where you're going or what your objective is, you'll end up somewhere you don't want to be. Keep your *why* clear and your motives will be pure.

2. Context
Having a clear *why* provides guiding principles as to what you

do and how you do it. It gives you context. Just as any great business plan includes core values, the call God placed on your life should define your direction. When you act purposefully, you eliminate the possibility of digression.

3. Endurance

I say it all the time. Ministry is messy. People are fickle. Leaders make mistakes. Budgets get cut. Suddenly your direct route has a major detour. When you find yourself in a time crunch or a sticky situation it's imperative to keep your *why* in the forefront of your mind. Clear purpose provides power and increases fortitude.

4. Experience

Many times we allow the gap between expectation and experience to overshadow day-to-day victories. Sometimes switching the lens through which you view what you are doing can actually alter your experience of it. When your *why* is clear, missteps translate into lessons learned, mistakes offer growth, and frustrations become nothing more than funny stories you tell at the staff Christmas party.

5. Courage

It's much easier to step out of the boat and onto the water when your eyes are on Jesus. Knowing and understanding your *why* will instill the courage to take the risks needed to achieve your vision.

We've all heard the famous Rosa Parks quote, "Stand for something or you will fall for anything." You may not realize the quote doesn't end there. Ms. Parks went on to say, "Today's mighty oak is yesterday's nut that held its ground." The latter part of her statement is my favorite because it promises results. When the daily grind of ministry wears me down, I start to lose sight of the calling God has placed on my life. It's much easier to focus on my to-do list rather than realign my heart with God's will and remind myself of the *why*.

My challenge for you today is that you refuse to work in vain. Don't allow the enemy to take your story hostage for even one

HOLD YOUR GROUND. STAND CONFIDENT IN YOUR CALLING AND KEEP THE WHY CLEAR AND PRESENT IN YOUR HEART.

day. Hold your ground. Stand confident in your calling and keep the *why* clear and present in your heart. To the outside world your *why* might seem small and insignificant, but I refuse to believe my calling is a side project. The Creator of the universe infused my heart with a passion for engaging kids and empowering families through Christ's love. I may look like a nut today, but I choose to believe my ministry will be a mighty oak tomorrow.

At the beginning of this book, we told the story of Helen Maroulis, an Olympic gold medalist. The part you might not remember is that, four years before her Olympic victory, Helen didn't even make the team. Even though she was ranked No. 1 in the United States, she was unexpectedly defeated by teammate Kelsey Campbell in the Olympic trials final. She was devastated and hurting, but the U.S. coach asked her to travel to the London Olympics as an assistant. No one would have blamed her for saying no. Yet she looked at the sport she loved and made the only decision she could make. London gave Helen the courage to regroup and refocus. In the 2016 Rio games, Helen defeated Saori Yoshida and won her long-awaited gold medal. Do you remember her words as she took the mat? "Christ in in me, I am enough."

Whatever your mission, wherever God has planted you, there is only One who can resurrect you when the weight of your calling feels like more than you can bear. The more you dwell on the struggles you face, the bigger they seem. Distraction for the sake of distraction isn't healthy, but diverting your attention with God's Word is highly recommended. If you need isolation, spend time meditating on God's promises instead of man's inadequacies. At the end of this chapter, you will find a list of some scripture references and worship songs we turn to when life gets hard. This race is a marathon, not a sprint. Your faithful obedience will require you to resurrect yourself time and time again in order to finish. Recall your *why* and refocus your passion. Remember God's past faithfulness in your life and begin to anticipate the journey He is taking you on. The best is yet to come. Don't Quit!

CHECK OUT THESE SCRIPTURES:

James 1:2-4	Isaiah 40:31
Hebrews 10:36	Galatians 6:9
Romans 5:3-4	1 Corinthians 9:24
Romans 15:13	Philippians 4:13
Romans 8:28	Hebrews 12:3

CHECK OUT THESE WORSHIP SONGS:

"10,000 Reasons"
by Matt Redman

"In Control"
by Hillsong Worship

"Broken Vessels"
by Hillsong Worship

"Jesus at the Center"
by Israel Houghton

"Do it Again"
by Elevation Worship

"Last Word"
by Elevation Worship

"Enough For Me"
by North Point InsideOut

"Resurrecting"
by Elevation Worship

"Here's my Heart"
by Lauren Daigle

"You're Bigger"
by Jekalyn Carr

"Holy"
by North Point InsideOut

"You're Never Gonna
Give Up On Me"
by Orange Kids Music

"I Can Do All Things"
by Orange Kids Music